Steck Vaughn

SCIENCE
Water Life

Joan S. Gottlieb

ISBN 0-7398-9178-2

5 6 7 8 862 11 10 09

Harcourt Achieve

Rigby • Steck-Vaughn

Contents

UNIT 1
Water Environments

All water environments are not the same.

Where there is water, there is life.

Properties of Water

Water is needed by all living things. You are made of **cells,** and your cells are mostly water. All other animals are made of cells, too. So are all plants. The cells of all animals and plants are mostly water. Many animals and plants actually live in or around water. In this book, you will read about many kinds of water life.

Why is water a good place for many plants and animals to live? Water has substances that plants and animals need. For example, oxygen and other gases are found mixed with, or dissolved in, water. Water animals take in the oxygen they need from the water as they breathe. Minerals are also dissolved in water. Water plants use the minerals to grow.

Water also provides a good home for many plants and animals because it changes temperature more slowly than air. In summer, water heats up slowly. It usually stays cooler than the hot summer air. In winter, water cools off slowly. It usually stays warmer than cold winter air. Animals and plants living in water are protected from great changes in temperature.

All water **environments** are not the same. An environment is a place where plants and animals live. In this unit, you will read about some different water environments. You will read also about some of the many kinds of plants and animals that live in these different water environments.

A. Fill in the missing words.

1. Water is needed by _____ living things. (some, all)

2. All animals are made of _____. (cells, plants)

3. Your cells are mostly _____. (air, water)

4. Oxygen and other gases are found mixed with, or _____, water. (melted in, dissolved in)

5. Water animals take in the _____ from water as they breathe. (minerals, oxygen)

6. Water plants use the _____ in water to grow. (minerals, oxygen)

7. Water changes temperature more _____ than air. (quickly, slowly)

8. All water environments are _____. (the same, not the same)

B. Answer True or False.

1. An environment is a place where plants and animals go for the winter. _____

2. Many animals and plants actually live in or around water. _____

3. Animals and plants living in water are protected from great changes in temperature. _____

4. Water has substances that animals and plants need. _____

C. Answer the question.

What happens to the temperature of water in the summer and winter?

_____

_____

_____

_____

Freshwater Environments

Trout swim in running water.

Water covers almost three fourths of Earth's surface. Most of this water is in the oceans. The water in oceans is **salt water.** Salt water has large amounts of dissolved salts. Water in streams, rivers, lakes, and ponds is **fresh water.** Fresh water does not have as much dissolved salt as ocean water.

Most plants and animals that live in ocean water cannot live in fresh water. Even different kinds of freshwater environments have different living things. There is running water in streams and rivers. Lakes and ponds have standing water.

Plants that grow in running water have roots that attach to the bottom of the river or stream. Animals that live in running water are fast swimmers, like trout. Or they may have **suckers.** A sucker is a part of an animal's body that attaches to rocks or to the bottom of a stream.

In a lake or pond, there are mosquitoes and other insects on the surface. Fish, frogs, turtles, and snakes live in standing water. Worms and clams can be found on the bottom. Plants like water lilies may float on the surface. Their roots are attached to the bottom. Animals like ducks and raccoons use lakes or ponds to find food.

A. Underline the correct words.

1. Water covers (almost three fourths, less than one fourth) of Earth's surface.

2. Most of Earth's water is in the (rivers, oceans).

3. The water in oceans is (fresh water, salt water).

4. Fresh water (has, does not have) as much dissolved salt as ocean water.

5. Most plants and animals that live in ocean water (cannot, can) live in fresh water.

6. There is running water in (lakes and ponds, streams and rivers).

7. (Lakes and ponds, Streams and rivers) have standing water.

8. Animals like ducks and raccoons use lakes or ponds to (swim, find food).

B. Write running water or standing water to tell where each plant or animal can be found.

1. mosquitoes _____

2. trout _____

3. turtles _____

4. water lilies _____

5. animals with suckers _____

C. Answer the questions.

1. How is fresh water different from ocean water? _____

_____

_____

2. How much of Earth's surface does water cover? _____

_____

Saltwater Environments

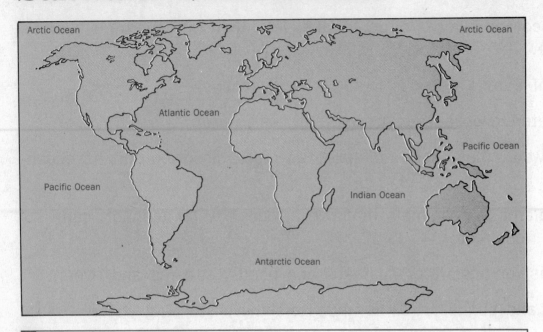

There are five oceans on Earth. They are the Atlantic, the Pacific, the Indian, the Arctic, and the Antarctic. Together, these oceans form a huge saltwater environment with many different kinds of living things.

On the surface of the oceans are tiny living things called **plankton.** Most plankton are too small to see without a microscope. Many saltwater animals feed on plankton.

The saltwater environment has many kinds of animals that swim about freely. Many of these animals are fish. There are more than 20,000 kinds of fish. They range in size from tiny dwarf gobies that are less than a half-inch long to whale sharks that can grow to be 59 feet long. Other animals that swim in the oceans are seals, whales, and octopuses.

Seaweeds live in shallow seawater. They cannot grow in deep water because they need sunlight to grow. Sunlight does not reach down into the deepest parts of oceans.

There are living things on the bottom of oceans, too. Animals like snails, starfish, crabs, and lobsters move along the ocean floor. Sponges and coral are animals that live attached to the ocean floor.

A. Write the names of the five oceans of Earth.

1. _____

2. _____

3. _____

4. _____

5. _____

B. Write the letter for the correct answer.

1. On the surface of oceans are tiny living things

   called _____.
   (a) seaweeds   (b) plankton   (c) fish

2. In the saltwater environment, most of the animals that swim about

   freely are _____.
   (a) fish   (b) crabs   (c) coral

3. _____ must live in shallow seawater.
   (a) Whales   (b) Octopuses   (c) Seaweeds

4. _____ are animals that live attached to the ocean floor.
   (a) Lobsters   (b) Seals   (c) Sponges and coral

C. Answer True or False.

1. There are five oceans on Earth. _____

2. Together, the oceans form a huge freshwater environment. _____

3. Sunlight can reach the deepest parts of oceans. _____

4. There are no living things on the bottom of oceans. _____

5. Many saltwater animals feed on plankton. _____

D. Answer the question.

Seaweeds cannot grow in deep water. Why? _____

_____

_____

Ocean Currents

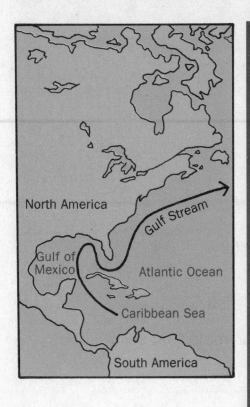

North America

Gulf Stream

Gulf of Mexico

Atlantic Ocean

Caribbean Sea

South America

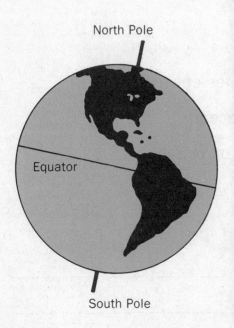

North Pole

Equator

South Pole

Oceans have **currents.** Currents are like rivers moving through the ocean waters. Some currents are warmer than the water around them. Others are colder. Currents move through oceans all over the world.

The two main kinds of currents are **surface currents** and **deep currents.** Most surface currents are caused by the wind. When wind moves surface water from a warm area of the ocean to a colder one, the current that forms is a warm one. A cold current forms when the wind moves cold water to a warm area of the ocean.

One of the best-known warm currents is the Gulf Stream. Find it on the map. The arrows show its path. The Gulf Stream moves north along the eastern coast of the United States. Then it travels northeast across the Atlantic Ocean toward England.

Deep currents are caused by differences in water temperature. Cold water is heavier than warm water. So, near the poles, cold water sinks to the ocean floor. As it moves toward the equator, it forms a deep current below the warm water.

Ocean currents affect the temperature of the nearby land. For example, the land areas near a warm current have a warmer climate because of the current.

Sometimes, deep currents come to the ocean's surface. These currents bring up minerals from the ocean floor. Plankton use these minerals to grow. Many kinds of fish and even whales feed on the plankton.

A. **Use the words below to complete the sentences.**

Currents	Gulf Stream	surface
Deep	Oceans	wind

1. _____ are like rivers moving through the ocean waters.

2. The two main kinds of currents are _____ currents and deep currents.

3. Most surface currents are caused by the _____ .

4. One of the best-known warm currents is the _____ .

5. _____ currents are caused by differences in water temperature.

B. **Use each pair of words to write a sentence about ocean currents.**

1. surface currents _____

_____

2. deep currents _____

_____

3. Gulf Stream _____

_____

C. **Answer True or False.**

1. Sometimes, deep currents come to the ocean's surface and bring up minerals from the ocean floor. _____

2. Currents only move through the Atlantic Ocean. _____

3. Plankton feed on many kinds of fish and even whales. _____

4. Ocean currents affect the temperature of nearby land. _____

5. Plankton use minerals to grow. _____

6. The Gulf Stream is a warm current. _____

Ocean Food Chains

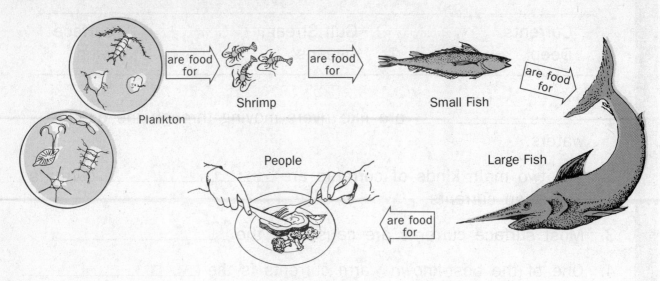

are food for

are food for

are food for

are food for

Plankton

Shrimp

Small Fish

Large Fish

People

An Ocean Food Chain

Small living things are often the food for bigger living things. These bigger living things are the food for even larger living things. The way that different living things depend on each other for food is called a **food chain.** There are food chains in both land environments and water environments.

Most food chains start with plants, because plants make their own food. To make food, plants need water, carbon dioxide gas, and the energy of sunlight. Animals cannot make food. Animals must eat plants or other animals for their food.

In oceans, plant plankton make their own food. They are the beginning of one kind of ocean food chain. The plant plankton are food for water animals, such as animal plankton. Animal plankton, in turn, are the food for bigger water animals, such as shrimp. The shrimp are eaten by small fish. The small fish are food for larger fish. People who eat these larger fish are part of this ocean food chain, too.

All ocean food chains do not follow the same path. There are many different food chains in the ocean. But most food chains, on land or in water, begin with plants. Only at the bottom of the ocean is this not true.

A. The living things listed below are part of an ocean food chain. Put them in the correct order. The first one is done for you.

_____ animal plankton

_____ shrimp

_____ small fish

___1___ plant plankton

_____ people

_____ large fish

B. Answer <u>True</u> or <u>False</u>.

1. The way that different living things depend on each other for food is called a food chain. _____

2. There are food chains only in land environments. _____

3. Plants make their own food. _____

4. To make food, plants need water, carbon dioxide gas, and the energy of sunlight. _____.

5. Animals make their own food. _____

6. All food chains, on land and in water, begin with large fish. _____

7. There are many different food chains in the ocean. _____

C. Answer the questions.

1. Why do most food chains start with plants? _____

_____

_____

2. How do animals get food? _____

_____

_____

Are Water Environments Important?

Water environments are important.

The cells of all animals and plants are mostly water. So without water, there could not be any life on Earth. But the water in cells is fresh water, not salt water. Could there be life on Earth without the saltwater oceans?

Remember that plant plankton in oceans make their own food. Plant plankton start ocean food chains that keep other living things alive. But plant plankton also give off oxygen as they make their food. Oxygen is used by people and other animals when they breathe. The oxygen in the air on Earth comes from plants. But most of the oxygen comes from ocean plants, not land plants.

Freshwater environments give many animals and plants the water they need to live. Saltwater environments provide most of the oxygen that animals and plants need to live. Are water environments important? What do you think?

Answer the questions.

1. Why are freshwater environments important? _____

_____

2. Why are saltwater environments important? _____

_____

Part A

Fill in the missing words.

1. The cells of all animals and plants are mostly _____. (water, air)

2. _____ is a place where plants and animals live. (A home, An environment)

3. The water in oceans is _____. (fresh water, salt water)

4. Fresh water does not have as much dissolved _____ as ocean water. (oxygen, salt)

5. On the surface of oceans are tiny living things called

   _____. (plankton, seaweeds)

6. One of the best-known warm _____ is the Gulf Stream. (oceans, currents)

7. The way that different things depend on each other for food is

   called _____. (plant plankton, a food chain)

8. Most food chains, on land and in water, start with _____. (animals, plants)

9. The oxygen in the air on Earth comes from _____. (animals, plants)

Part B

Read each sentence. Write <u>True</u> if the sentence is true. Write <u>False</u> if the sentence is false.

1. The land areas near a warm ocean current have a warm climate.

   _____

2. Most of the water on Earth is in the oceans. _____

3. All water environments are the same. _____

4. Shrimp and larger fish start ocean food chains. _____

5. Most of the oxygen in the air comes from ocean plants. _____

EXPLORE & DISCOVER

Make an Ocean Environment

You Need

- a partner
- butcher paper
- masking tape
- paints
- blue glitter
- glue
- sand
- disposable containers
- water

1. Work with your partner to create an underwater ocean environment.

2. Make an underwater ocean background by painting the butcher paper blue. Leave room at the bottom for the ocean floor.

3. Make the ocean floor along the bottom of the paper. Use dark colors to paint rocks. Mix equal amounts of glue and water. Add enough brown paint to make a sandy color. Use the mixture to paint the ocean floor. Sprinkle it lightly with sand before the paint dries.

4. To show that the water moves, paint wavy marks and bubbles using shades of blue and green paint. Sprinkle blue glitter on it before the paint dries.

5. Tape your background on the wall and save it so you can add life to it later.

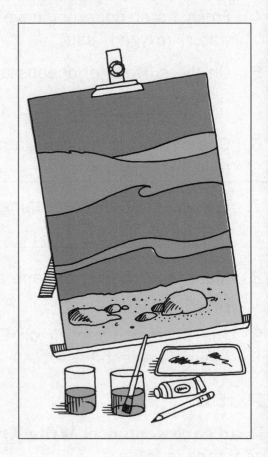

Write the Answer

What ocean are you interested in studying? What do you think lives there?

_____

_____

_____

Fill in the circle in front of the word or phrase that best completes each sentence. The first one is done for you.

1. Almost three fourths of Earth's surface is
   ⓐ air.
   ● water.
   ⓒ land.

2. A place where plants and animals live is called
   ⓐ a food chain.
   ⓑ a current.
   ⓒ an environment.

3. Compared with fresh water, ocean water has more
   ⓐ plants.
   ⓑ animals.
   ⓒ salt.

4. On the surface of oceans, there are tiny
   ⓐ crabs.
   ⓑ plankton.
   ⓒ starfish.

5. The cells of all animals and plants are mostly
   ⓐ water.
   ⓑ minerals.
   ⓒ salt.

6. Streams and rivers have
   ⓐ standing water.
   ⓑ running water.
   ⓒ salt water.

Fill in the missing words.

7. Most food chains begin with _____. (water, plants)

8. Plant plankton give off _____.
   (oxygen, carbon dioxide)

9. The Gulf Stream is _____. (a current, an ocean)

Write the answer on the lines.

10. What kind of water is in streams, rivers, lakes, and ponds?

_____

_____

UNIT 2
Water Plants

Kelp

Red Algae

Algae

The largest group of underwater organisms that make their own food is called **algae.** Algae live in oceans, rivers, lakes, and ponds. Algae have no roots, stems, leaves, or flowers and are not plants. But like plants, algae have **chlorophyll,** which is the green matter that helps plants to make their own food.

Some algae are so small that they can be seen only under a microscope. Other algae, such as seaweeds, can grow to be very large. Algae are usually grouped by color. There are green, brown, red, and blue-green algae. However, most scientists consider blue-green algae to be more like bacteria.

Green algae are often found in fresh water. Large amounts of these algae can make an entire lake turn green. Many green algae are tiny one-celled organisms that are food for fish and other animals that live in the water.

Kelp is a kind of large brown algae that can grow to be 200 feet long. It has ribbonlike blades that float in the ocean. Some kelps have parts called holdfasts that hold the blades to rocks. Algin, a substance found in kelp, is used to thicken many products, such as ice cream, puddings, and cosmetics.

Most red algae are small and delicate. More kinds of red algae live in the ocean than in fresh water. Red algae can live on the shore where ocean waves break or almost 2 miles below the ocean's surface. People in Japan grow red algae and then dry it to make a food called nori.

A. Fill in the missing words.

1. The _____ group of underwater organisms that make their own food is called algae. (largest, smallest)

2. Algae have _____ roots, stems, leaves, or flowers. (no, many)

3. Algae are usually grouped by _____. (where they grow, color)

4. Green algae are often found in _____ water. (salt, fresh)

5. Most red algae are _____ and delicate. (small, large)

6. Kelp has ribbonlike _____. (stems, blades)

B. Answer True or False.

1. Algae live in oceans, rivers, lakes, and ponds. _____

2. Algae do not have chlorophyll. _____

3. All algae are so small they can be seen only under a microscope.

   _____

4. Large amounts of green algae can make an entire lake turn orange.

   _____

5. Kelp is a large brown algae that can grow to be 200 feet long.

   _____

6. Blue-green algae are more like bacteria than plants. _____

7. Red algae cannot live below the ocean's surface. _____

8. Many green algae are tiny, one-celled organisms. _____

C. Draw lines to match each kind of algae with its description.

1. kelp   dried to make nori

2. red algae   brown algae that can be 200 feet long

3. green algae   more like bacteria than plants

4. blue-green algae   food for fish and other water animals

19

Duckweed

Duckweed grows very fast and can clog canals and waterways.

One group of water plants is called **duckweed.** It provides food for many ducks and other water birds. Large goldfish also feed on duckweed.

Duckweed is a **perennial.** That means it lives year after year. Duckweed has no true leaves or stems. But some kinds of duckweed have **fronds,** or leaflike parts, that float on the surface of ponds. Hairlike roots anchor the fronds to the muddy bottom. Other kinds of duckweed are small and float on the surface. Duckweed has tiny flowers. In fact, one kind of duckweed is the smallest flowering plant known. The flowers and fruits of most kinds of duckweed are so small they are difficult to see.

Duckweed plants can grow in **temperate climates,** which have cold winters and warm summers. In winter, duckweed plants form buds that are released into the water and drop to the muddy bottom. The mud keeps the buds from freezing. When spring comes and the mud heats up, the duckweed buds send new plants to the surface.

In **tropical climates,** where it is warm all year, duckweed grows very fast. It clogs canals and waterways. This can be a danger to boats.

A. Answer True or False.

1. Duckweed is a perennial water plant. _____

2. Large goldfish feed on duckweed. _____

3. Duckweed plants have many leaves and stems. _____

4. Some kinds of duckweed are small and float on the surface.

   _____

5. Duckweed is the largest flowering plant known. _____

6. Duckweed can grow in temperate and tropical climates. _____

B. Use the words below to complete the sentences.

boats	fronds	plants
buds	fruits	temperate
ducks	mud	tropical

1. Duckweed provides food for many _____ and other water birds.

2. The flowers and _____ of most kinds of duckweed are so small they are difficult to see.

3. In winter, duckweed plants form _____ that are released into the water and drop to the muddy bottom.

4. Some kinds of duckweed have _____, or leaflike parts.

5. In winter, _____ keeps duckweed buds from freezing.

6. When spring comes and the mud heats up, the duckweed buds send new _____ to the surface.

7. Duckweed can grow in _____ climates, which have cold winters and warm summers.

8. In _____ climates, duckweed grows very fast.

9. Duckweed clogs canals and waterways, which can be a danger to

   _____ .

Water Lilies

Water Lilies

Victoria Water Lily

Water lilies are large perennial water plants. They grow year after year in lakes, ponds, and slow-moving streams. Water lilies grow in both temperate and tropical climates. Their roots cling to the bottom of the pond or stream. The roots send flower and leaf stalks up from the muddy bottom.

Water lilies have large, round, green leaves that float on or just below the surface of the water. The Victoria lily, in South America, has leaves that can be more than 5 feet across. The leaves have turned-up edges and look like big pie pans.

Water lilies have beautiful flowers. The white-flowered water lily is the most common. But other kinds may have yellow, pink, red, or blue flowers. The Australian water lily has beautiful purplish-blue flowers that can grow to be 12 inches wide. Water lily flowers are usually held above the water on a strong stalk. Some water lilies bloom during the day, but others bloom only at night.

The fruit of the water lily is like a berry filled with seeds. Often the fruit ripens underwater. Then it bursts open and the seeds float away or sink. New roots grow from the seeds. Water lilies grow very fast. Sometimes, they grow so thick that they block waterways and can become a danger to boats.

A. Answer True or False.

1. Water lilies grow year after year in salty ocean water. _____

2. Water lily flowers are held above the water on a strong stalk.

   _____

3. The fruit of the water lily often ripens underwater. _____

4. All water lilies bloom only at night. _____

5. The fruit of the water lily has no seeds. _____

6. Water lilies grow only in tropical climates. _____

B. Fill in the missing words.

1. Water lilies have roots that cling to the _____ of the pond or stream. (bottom, surface)

2. The fruit of the water lily is like a berry filled with _____ . (seeds, water)

3. Water lilies have _____, round, green leaves that float on or just below the surface of the water. (large, small)

4. The Victoria Lily, in South America, has leaves that can be more

   than _____ feet across. (25, 5)

5. Water lilies grow very _____ . (fast, slowly)

6. Water lilies have beautiful flowers that come in _____ one color. (only, more than)

C. The sentences below tell how water lilies start new plants. Put the sentences in the correct order. The first one is done for you.

_____ The fruit bursts open.

___1___ Often the fruit ripens underwater.

_____ The seeds float away or sink.

_____ New roots grow from the seeds.

_____ New leaves and flowers grow up from the roots.

Mangroves

Young Mangrove Trees

Mangroves are trees that grow in salt water. They grow best in warm, wet places along coastlines and at the edges of marshes and rivers. Mangrove trees have thick, oval leaves and large, yellow flowers.

The main roots of mangrove trees anchor the tree in soft mud. Other roots grow out of mangrove stems like downward branches. These roots act as stilts and keep the trunk of the tree out of water.

Often leaves and other materials get caught in the roots. These materials build up and make more soil. They may build up so much soil that it becomes dry land. Then the mangroves die because they can no longer reach water.

Mangrove seeds are 6 to 8 inches long. The seeds may sprout while they are still on the tree. Then they fall into the water. Some seeds float for months in the water. When waves push them into shallow, still water, roots grow down into the mud. Mangrove seeds can send roots down as far as a foot to reach mud and start new trees.

There are different kinds of mangroves. In Everglades National Park in Florida, some mangroves grow as high as 70 feet. Red mangroves grow from the coast of Florida all the way to South America. They grow to be about 25 feet high.

Mangrove wood is hard and heavy. In tropical countries it is used in construction and burned for fuel. People also use the bark for making dyes and tanning leather.

A. Answer True or False.

1. Mangrove seeds are 6 to 8 inches long. _____

2. The roots of mangrove trees anchor the tree in mud. _____

3. Some mangrove seeds float for months in the water. _____

4. Mangrove wood is soft and light. _____

5. Mangrove trees have small white flowers. _____

B. Write the letter for the correct answer.

1. Mangroves grow in _____ .
   (a) fresh water   (b) gravel   (c) salt water

2. Mangroves are found in _____ .
   (a) wet places   (b) dry places   (c) high places

3. The roots that keep the trunk out of water act as _____ .
   (a) balloons   (b) stilts   (c) mud

4. Red mangroves grow from the coast of Florida all the way to _____ .
   (a) Canada   (b) Central America   (c) South America

5. People use the bark of mangrove trees for making dyes and _____ .
   (a) tanning leather   (b) glass   (c) mud

6. Mangrove seeds can send roots down to mud as far as a _____ .
   (a) foot   (b) mile   (c) yard

C. The sentences below tell how mangrove trees start new trees. Put the sentences in the correct order. The first one is done for you.

_____ Then the seeds fall into the water.

_____ The roots grow down into the mud.

_____ Some seeds float for months in the water.

___1___ Seeds sprout while they are still on the tree.

_____ Waves push the seeds into shallow, still water.

_____ Mangrove seeds start new trees.

Bald Cypresses

The knees of bald cypress trees grow out of the water, around the tree trunk.

The **bald cypress** is a tree that grows in wet areas from Texas to New Jersey. It can reach a height of 170 feet.

The crowns, or tops, of bald cypresses are usually large. They may be 100 feet across. Bald cypresses have light green leaves and cone-shaped trunks.

Bald cypresses look a lot like pine trees. They have seeds that form in cones. Bald cypresses also have flat, needlelike leaves, just like pine trees.

But bald cypresses shed their leaves, or needles, every year and pine trees do not. Bald cypress needles begin to turn orange in the fall. Every winter the needles, and even young twigs, die and fall off the tree. Then the tree is bald.

The roots of the bald cypress spread out under the water. These roots produce growths called **knees** that look like human knees. The knees can grow to be about 6 feet tall. They grow out of the water around the tree trunk. People sometimes cut off the knees and polish them to make decorations. If too many knees are cut off, the tree dies.

Underline the correct words.

1. The bald cypress is a tree that grows in (wet, dry) areas.

2. Bald cypresses have seeds that form in (flowers, cones).

3. Every winter, the needles and even young (twigs, birds) die and fall off the tree.

4. The roots produce growths called (elbows, knees).

Part A

Fill in the missing words.

1. The green matter that helps plants to make their own food is

   _____. (seaweed, chlorophyll)

2. Large amounts of green algae can make an entire lake

   _____. (dry up, turn green)

3. Bald cypresses have flat, needlelike _____. (roots, leaves)

4. One kind of plant that provides food for ducks and other water birds

   is _____. (duckweed, bald cypress)

5. A large brown algae with ribbonlike blades is _____.
   (kelp, red algae)

6. Bald cypresses are a lot like _____ trees. (maple, pine)

7. The mangrove has roots that act as _____. (balloons, stilts)

8. Mangroves grow only in _____. (fresh water, salt water)

9. Algae are usually grouped by _____. (size, color)

Part B

Choose the word or words that best match each plant to its use.

duckweed	kelp	red algae
green algae	mangroves	water lilies

1. food for ducks and large goldfish _____

2. dyes and tanning leather _____

3. tiny food for fish _____

4. algin from this algae thickens some products _____

5. dried to make nori _____

Make Ocean Environment Plants

You Need

- a partner
- brown paper bags
- glue or clear tape
- green tissue paper
- scissors
- encyclopedia or books on oceans

1. Use the underwater ocean world you made in Unit 1. Choose an ocean environment for your world to be. Use books or encyclopedias to research the plant and animal life that live there.

2. The most common underwater organisms that make their own food are algae, or seaweed. Find out what kinds of seaweed grow in your ocean.

3. Make some algae for your ocean. Use the chart to see what some seaweeds look like. Green tissue paper can make sea lettuce. Brown paper bags can be used to make ribbons of kelp.

4. Seaweed attaches itself to rocks on the ocean floor. Can you find out why?

5. Use tape or glue to attach your plants to the rocks and water background.

Common Seaweeds	
Rockweed (green)	
Sea Lettuce (green)	
Sargassum (brown)	
Horsetail Kelp (brown)	
Irish Moss (green-purple)	

Write the Answer

Water plants are very important to animals. Explain why this is so.

_____

_____

_____

Fill in the circle in front of the word or phrase that best completes each sentence. The first one is done for you.

1. The largest group of underwater organisms with chlorophyll is
   ● algae.
   ⓑ duckweed.
   ⓒ mangroves.

2. There are four kinds of algae: brown, red, blue-green, and
   ⓐ purple.
   ⓑ orange.
   ⓒ green.

3. Mangroves grow in
   ⓐ salt water.
   ⓑ fresh water.
   ⓒ other trees.

4. One water plant that provides food for ducks is
   ⓐ algae.
   ⓑ duckweed.
   ⓒ bald cypress.

5. Many water lily fruits ripen
   ⓐ in sand.
   ⓑ underwater.
   ⓒ in ice.

6. Bald cypresses have growths called knees that grow
   ⓐ down into the mud.
   ⓑ out of the treetops.
   ⓒ out of the water.

Fill in the missing words.

7. Mangrove roots catch leaves and other materials that create

   _____ soil. (more, less)

8. The leaves of a bald cypress tree look like _____. (needles, feathers)

9. Bald cypress trees grow in _____. (the sand, wet areas)

Write the answer on the lines.

10. Explain where water lilies grow.

   _____

   _____

UNIT 3
Invertebrate Water Animals

What Is an Invertebrate?

Sea Urchin

When you think of animals, you probably think of animals with backbones. People, cows, and dogs are animals with backbones. Some animals with backbones, such as fish, turtles, and frogs, live in or around water. Animals with backbones are called **vertebrates.** They are called vertebrates because the bones that make up backbones are called **vertebrae.**

Most animals on Earth are not vertebrates. Most animals are **invertebrates.** Invertebrates are animals that do not have backbones. Spiders, flies, and worms are examples of invertebrate animals. There are more than one million kinds of invertebrates.

Many kinds of invertebrates live in water. Sea urchins, shrimp, and squid are some examples. Most invertebrate water animals are smaller than vertebrates. Some are so small that you need a microscope to see them. Invertebrates are the simplest of all animals. Most have only a few parts. Some invertebrates have no tissues, body systems, or organs.

A. Fill in the missing words.

1. Animals with backbones are called _____.
(vertebrates, invertebrates)

2. _____ are animals that do not have backbones.
(Vertebrates, Invertebrates)

3. Most animals on Earth are _____.
(vertebrates, invertebrates)

4. Most invertebrate water animals are _____ than vertebrates.
(bigger, smaller)

5. Invertebrates are the _____ of all animals.
(most dangerous, simplest)

6. Three examples of invertebrates are spiders, flies, and

_____. (worms, birds)

B. Write vertebrate or invertebrate after the names of the animals.

1. dogs _____

2. spiders _____

3. squid _____

4. people _____

5. fish _____

C. Answer True or False.

1. The bones that make up backbones are called vertebrae. _____

2. Some invertebrates are so small you need a microscope to see

them. _____

3. There are fewer than two thousand invertebrates. _____

4. Some invertebrates have no tissues, body systems, or organs.

_____

Snails

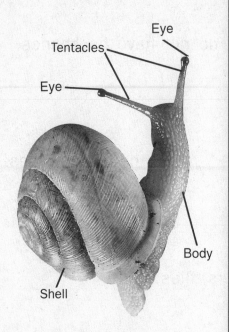

Eye

Tentacles

Eye

Body

Shell

Freshwater Snail

Saltwater Snail

The largest group of invertebrate water animals is called **mollusks.** All mollusks have soft bodies. Many of them have shells that protect their soft bodies. There are six main groups, or classes, of mollusks. Some have one or two parts to their shells, others have more. Many mollusks have no shells at all.

Snails are mollusks with one-part shells. Snails are found in fresh water and in salt water. Most snails have two **tentacles.** Tentacles are feelers that stick out from their heads. The tentacles have eyes on them.

Some freshwater snails have **gills.** Gills let fish and other water animals take in oxygen that is dissolved in water. Other freshwater snails have lungs. These snails must come to the surface of the water often to get the oxygen they need. Some freshwater snails feed on algae. They eat by grinding food with their tongues. There are thousands of tiny teeth on their tongues.

Many saltwater snails have cone-shaped shells. These ocean snails have a long tube. The tube takes in water. The water passes over the gills. The gills take oxygen out of the water for the snails to breathe. Ocean snails also have two tentacles with eyes on the ends.

Cone-shaped snails do not eat plants. They eat other water animals, such as worms, smaller mollusks, and tiny fish. They have a poison sac, or pouch, hooked to their teeth. They can poison an animal so it cannot move. Then they eat it.

A. Use the words below to answer the questions.

algae	lungs	poison	snails
gills	mollusks	shells	tentacles

1. What is the largest group of invertebrate water animals called?

   _____

2. What do most mollusks have that protect their soft bodies?

   _____

3. What mollusks have one-part shells? _____

4. What lets fish and other water animals take in oxygen that is

   dissolved in water? _____

5. What do some freshwater snails feed on? _____

6. A snail's eyes are on what part of the snail? _____

7. What do cone-shaped snails have in their sacs? _____

B. Write freshwater, saltwater, or both to answer the questions.

1. Which snails feed on algae? _____

2. Which snails are mollusks? _____

3. Which snails have a poison sac? _____

4. Which snails have eyes on their tentacles? _____

5. Which snails have cone-shaped shells? _____

6. Which snails have one-part shells? _____

C. Answer the question.

What can cone-shaped snails do when they eat an animal? _____

_____

_____

Clams

Giant Clam

Clams are mollusks that have shells with two parts. The two parts are held together by hard tissue called a **ligament.** The ligament acts like a hinge. It opens and closes the shell.

Clams live in saltwater and freshwater environments. They dig into sandy ocean beaches. They live on the muddy bottoms of oceans, ponds, and rivers in many parts of the world. The giant clams that live near Australia have 4-foot-long shells that can weigh 500 pounds.

A clam has a **foot,** which is a muscle under its body. The foot helps the clam to move. It also acts as an anchor to keep the clam in one place. If a clam is touched gently, it may use its foot like a shovel. It quickly digs itself under the sand. Hiding is one way a clam protects itself from animals that feed on clams.

How else can a clam protect itself? Remember, a clam has a ligament that can close the two parts of its shell. Other water animals want to eat the soft body of the clam, not the hard shell. If other animals are about to attack, a clam uses its ligament to snap its shell tightly shut.

Two tubes stick out of the clam from the end that is opposite its foot. Water is sucked into one tube. The water carries bits of plants and animals that the clam eats. The water also carries oxygen. The clam has gills that help get the dissolved oxygen out of the water. The other tube pushes out water that carries waste materials from the clam.

A. **Write the letter for the correct answer.**

1. Clams are mollusks that have _____ .
   (a) six shells   (b) shells with two parts   (c) no shells

2. The shell parts of a clam are held together by a _____ .
   (a) ligament   (b) gill   (c) foot

3. Clams live in _____ environments.
   (a) only freshwater   (b) only saltwater   (c) both a and b

4. A clam has a _____ , which is a muscle under its body.
   (a) ligament   (b) gill   (c) foot

B. **Choose the word or words that best match the body parts of a clam with the job they do.**

foot	ligament	tentacles
gills	shell	tubes

1. help get dissolved oxygen out of the water _____

2. suck in and push out water _____

3. helps the clam to move _____

4. opens and closes the shell _____

5. shuts if other animals are about to attack _____

C. **Answer the questions.**

1. What are two uses for a clam's foot? _____

_____

_____

_____

2. What is one way a clam protects itself? _____

_____

_____

Octopuses

An octopus has eight arms, called tentacles.

An octopus is a mollusk that has no shell at all. It looks as if it is all head and arms. An octopus has eight arms, called tentacles, which have many suckers on them. Suckers hold on tightly to objects they touch. The suckers help an octopus to crawl and to hold on to its food.

An octopus moves by pulling itself along by its tentacles. It can also use a kind of jet propulsion to move. It pulls in water through its gills and sends it out very fast through a tube under its head. The force of the water moves the octopus backward.

One way that an octopus can find food is by hiding among stones and seashells on the ocean floor. The octopus can change its color to match its surroundings. Small water animals that swim by usually do not see the octopus. The octopus can grab an animal with its tentacles.

Most kinds of octopuses are as small as a person's fist. How do they escape bigger animals that feed on them? An octopus can squirt out a liquid, like ink, that blackens the water. The octopus then swims away. Giant octopuses that live in the Pacific Ocean have few enemies to swim away from. These octopuses can grow to be 30 feet long.

A. Answer True or False.

1. An octopus is a mollusk that has no shell at all. _____

2. An octopus has eight arms, called tentacles. _____

3. An octopus does not use its tentacles to help it move. _____

4. Suckers hold on tightly to objects they touch. _____

5. An octopus does not have gills. _____

6. An octopus cannot change its color to match its surroundings.

   _____

7. An octopus can squirt out a black ink that other water animals like to drink. _____

8. Giant octopuses can grow to be 30 feet long. _____

9. An octopus feeds on small water plants. _____

B. Answer the questions.

1. What are two ways an octopus can move? _____

   _____

   _____

2. How do suckers help an octopus? _____

   _____

   _____

C. Use each word to write a sentence about octopuses.

1. color _____

   _____

2. tentacles _____

   _____

3. ink _____

   _____

37

Starfish

The Tube Feet of a Starfish

This starfish has begun to attach its tube feet to a clam.

Starfish live in all oceans. *Fish* is part of their name, but they are not fish. They are invertebrates. Starfish have a small central body, with a mouth on the bottom side. Most starfish have five arms that stick out from their bodies. Other kinds have more than 25 arms. Stiff spines cover their bodies and arms. Starfish are often dull yellow or orange but can be bright colors, too. They can be as small as $\frac{1}{2}$ inch and as big as 3 feet wide.

Starfish use their tube feet to move. These small tube feet are under each arm. Suction cups are attached to the feet. The suction cups help starfish to move.

Starfish eat animals. They especially like clams and other mollusks. A starfish catches a clam with its arms. The clam closes its shell to protect itself. Using its tube feet, the starfish forces the shell open a little bit. Then the starfish turns its stomach inside out and pushes it out of its mouth. It sticks its stomach into the opened clamshell and eats the soft clam body. Then the starfish pulls its stomach out of the clam and puts it back into its own body.

A starfish can grow new arms if its arms are broken off. In fact, if a starfish loses all its arms but one and most of its central body, a new body and new arms will grow. Starfish eat mollusks like clams and oysters that are valuable crops for fishermen. The fishermen may try to destroy starfish by cutting them into pieces. But the pieces grow into even more starfish.

A. Underline the correct words.

1. Starfish are found in (some oceans and rivers, all oceans).

2. Most starfish have (one arm, five arms).

3. Starfish use their (tube feet, stiff spines) to move.

4. Starfish eat (plants, animals).

5. If a starfish is cut into pieces,
   (the starfish dies, the pieces grow into more starfish).

B. The steps below describe how a starfish eats a clam. Number the steps in the correct order. The first one is done for you.

_____ The starfish pushes its stomach out of its mouth.

_____ The starfish eats the soft clam body.

___1___ A starfish catches a clam with its arms.

_____ The starfish puts its stomach back into its own body.

_____ The clam closes its shell.

_____ The starfish sticks its stomach into the clamshell.

_____ The starfish forces the shell open a little bit.

C. Answer True or False.

1. Starfish can be 3 feet wide. _____

2. Some starfish have more than 25 arms. _____

3. Starfish are often black or gray. _____

4. A starfish can grow new arms if its arms are broken off.

   _____

5. Suction cups are attached to a starfish's stomach. _____

D. Answer the question.

What happens if a starfish is cut into pieces? _____

_____

Crabs

The blue crab is a crab that people eat.

Crabs belong to a group of water animals called **crustaceans.** Animals in this group have shells. They also have **segmented bodies.** Segmented bodies are bodies made of separate parts that are joined together.

Most crabs have five pairs of jointed legs. A jointed leg has several separate parts joined together. Four pairs of legs are used for walking on rocks and on land. Although crabs can move in any direction, they usually move sideways. The fifth and back pair of legs is used for swimming. These legs are often flat like paddles. The two front legs have claws. Crabs use their claws for catching food and for fighting enemies.

As a crab grows, it **molts.** When it molts, it loses its shell. Then it grows a new, larger shell. At the time a crab molts, it can also grow a new leg or claw if it has lost one. In fact, if some enemy is holding on to a crab's leg, the crab can separate itself from the leg. Then, when the crab molts again, it grows a brand-new leg.

There are many different kinds of crabs. Most crabs live in oceans, but some live in fresh water. The pea crab is so tiny that it lives inside the shell of an oyster. The giant spider crab of Japan has legs that are 4 feet long.

Crabs eat other small crustaceans and plant life. In turn, crabs are eaten by many vertebrate animals. People use several kinds of crabs for food.

A. Use the words below to complete the sentences.

crustaceans	molting	segmented
legs	oceans	swimming
mollusks	plant	walking

1. Crabs belong to a group of water animals called

   _____ .

2. Crustaceans have _____ bodies, which are made of separate parts that are joined together.

3. Most crabs have five pairs of jointed _____ .

4. Four pairs of a crab's legs are used for _____ .

5. The crab's back pair of legs is used for _____ .

6. The process of shedding a shell and growing a new one is called

   _____ .

7. Most crabs live in _____ .

8. Crabs eat other small crustaceans and _____ life.

B. Answer the questions.

1. What do crabs use their claws for? _____

   _____

2. If an enemy is holding on to a crab's leg, what can the crab do?

   _____

   _____

   _____

C. Use the word to write a sentence about crabs.

molting _____

_____

Lobsters

American Lobster

Lobsters belong to the crustacean group of animals. Lobsters are found only in salt water. The segmented body of a lobster is divided into 21 segments. A lobster has five pairs of jointed legs. Four pairs are used for crawling along the ocean bottom. The other two legs end in large claws, one slightly bigger than the other. A lobster uses its claws to catch and tear apart small fish and mollusks that it eats.

Like crabs, lobsters molt. Lobsters can also grow a new leg if one breaks off. A lobster's eyes are on stems that stick out from its head. A lobster cannot move its head, but it can move the stems. A lobster has 20 pairs of gills. With its gills, the lobster gets the oxygen it needs from water.

The American lobster is dark green on top and orange or blue underneath. This is the kind of lobster that many Americans eat. At one time, so many lobsters were being caught that they became endangered. Today, laws protect lobsters.

Answer True or False.

1. Lobsters belong to the crustacean group of animals. _____

2. A lobster has five pairs of jointed legs. _____

3. There are no laws to protect lobsters. _____

Sea Anemones

Have you ever seen flowers called anemones? There are water animals that look like these flowers. These animals are called sea anemones. They belong to a group of invertebrate water animals known as **coelenterates.** Some of the world's most colorful and beautiful sea animals are coelenterates.

A sea anemone has many tentacles, or arms. The tentacles have special cells with poison in them. The sea anemone stings passing tiny fish or crustaceans with its tentacles. Then, the tentacles take the food into the sea anemone's mouth.

Sea anemones can be found everywhere in the oceans. Most of them live along the seacoast, where they attach themselves to rocks and shells.

A sea anemone catches its food.

A. Fill in the missing words.

1. Sea anemones belong to a group of invertebrate water animals known as _____. (crustaceans, coelenterates)

2. A sea anemone has many _____. (tentacles, claws)

3. Sea anemones can be found everywhere in _____. (oceans, rivers)

B. Answer the question.

How do sea anemones use their tentacles to get food? _____

_____

_____

_____

43

Coral Animals

Two Coral Colonies

Like sea anemones, coral animals are coelenterates. But unlike sea anemones, coral animals have **skeletons.** Skeletons are frameworks that support a body. Coral animals are usually less than 1 inch wide. At one end of a coral animal's body is a mouth. Tiny tentacles stick out from around the mouth. The tentacles catch even tinier plankton, which the coral animals feed on.

Coral animals live together in a **colony,** or group. They attach themselves to each other by thin tissue. A coral colony can be very big. As coral animals reproduce, the older ones die. Their skeletons stay where they are, and new coral animals attach themselves to the skeletons. As time passes, the colony grows. Colonies can grow in different shapes. Some look like heads of cabbage, and others look like trees without leaves.

Coral colonies grow only in warm salt water. They can be found, for example, in the South Pacific Ocean and in the Caribbean Sea. Many colonies can grow together to make a wall, called a **coral reef.** A reef can go all the way from the bottom of the ocean to the surface of the water. The Great Barrier Reef off the coast of Australia is the world's largest coral reef. It is about 1,250 miles long.

A. Write the letter for the correct answer.

1. Coral animals are _____.
   (a) coelenterates   (b) sea anemones   (c) plants

2. Tiny _____ stick out from around the mouth of a coral animal.
   (a) plankton   (b) skeletons   (c) tentacles

3. Coral animals live together in a _____.
   (a) skeleton   (b) coelenterate   (c) colony

4. Coral colonies grow only in _____.
   (a) warm salt water   (b) cold water   (c) fresh water

5. Many coral colonies can grow together to make a coral _____.
   (a) ocean   (b) reef   (c) skeleton

B. Answer True or False.

1. Unlike sea anemones, coral animals have skeletons. _____

2. The skeletons of coral animals catch even tinier plankton.

   _____

3. The Great Barrier Reef is off the coast of America. _____

4. Coral colonies always grow in the same shape. _____

5. A coral reef can go all the way from the bottom of the ocean to the

   surface of the water. _____

6. Some coral animals look like heads of cabbage, and others look like

   trees without leaves. _____

C. The steps below describe how coral colonies grow. Number the steps in the correct order. The first one is done for you.

_____ New coral animals attach themselves to the skeletons.

_____ As time passes, the colony grows.

__1__ Coral animals attach themselves to each other.

_____ The skeletons of dead coral animals stay where they are.

_____ As coral animals reproduce, the older ones die.

Jellyfish

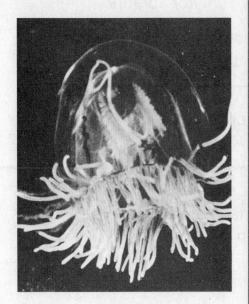

A Jellyfish

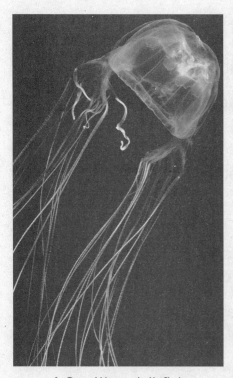

A Sea Wasp Jellyfish

Jellyfish belong to the coelenterate group of invertebrate water animals. The jellyfish gets its name from the fact that inside its body is a material that looks like jelly. The jellyfish's body is almost transparent. This means you can look through its body and see the jellylike material inside. Jellyfish are often very colorful and beautiful.

The jellyfish is an animal that has no brain. It spends most of its life moving slowly through the water. Jellyfish move by drawing water in and pushing water out of their bodies at a steady pace. This keeps them from sinking into the deep sea where they would soon die.

Most jellyfish have long, stinging tentacles that hang down from their body. They use their tentacles to trap small sea animals swimming by. The jellyfish stings the small sea animals with a strong poison from its tentacles. The jellyfish then passes the poisoned animal to its mouth, which is at the center of its body.

There are many kinds of jellyfish. Some can have bodies that are only 1 inch wide. Others, like the great red jellyfish, can grow to be 7 feet wide, with 100-foot-long tentacles.

Many jellyfish are free-swimming, but some do not swim through the ocean waters. These attach themselves to rock or coral with a stalk.

The poison of some jellyfish is very dangerous. Sea wasps live north of Australia. They are small but their stings can kill a person.

A. **Use the words below to complete the sentences.**

animals	colorful	jellyfish
brain	invertebrate	tentacles

1. Jellyfish belong to the coelenterate group of _____ water animals.

2. Jellyfish are often very _____ and beautiful.

3. The jellyfish is an animal that has no _____ .

4. Most jellyfish have long, stinging _____ that hang down from their body.

5. Jellyfish use their tentacles to trap small sea _____ .

B. **Answer the questions.**

1. How does the jellyfish get its name? _____

   _____

   _____

2. How does a jellyfish move? _____

   _____

   _____

C. **Answer** <u>True</u> **or** <u>False</u>**.**

1. You can look through the body of a jellyfish and see the jellylike

   material inside. _____

2. There is only one kind of jellyfish. _____

3. All jellyfish are free swimming animals that swim through

   the ocean waters. _____

4. It is dangerous to touch a dead sea wasp on a beach.

   _____ .

Sponges

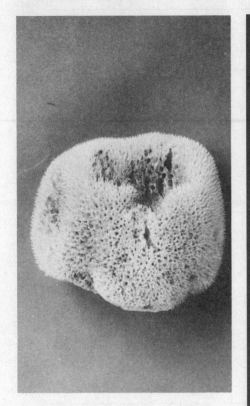

There are more than 4,500 kinds of sponges.

You may have used a sponge to wash a car or to clean something in your home. The sponge you used was probably made in a factory. But some sponges people use are real sponges from the sea. They are the skeletons of a tiny sea animal.

There are more than 4,500 kinds of sponges. They are found mainly in warm, shallow ocean water. They attach themselves to the bottom or to rocks. Because sponges move so little, people might think they are plants. They even look like plants. But sponges are animals. They have soft skeletons that easily absorb, or soak up, water. After these sponges are collected and dried, they can be used for cleaning.

Some sponges grow in colonies. Whether colonies of sponges or single sponges, they can be as small as the head of a pin or can grow to be 6 feet tall. They grow in many different shapes, and some have bright colors.

Underline the correct words.

1. Some sponges that people use are the skeletons of a tiny sea (animal, plant).

2. Because sponges move so little, people might think they are (animals, plants).

3. Sponges are found in warm (shallow, deep) ocean water.

4. Sponges have (soft, hard) skeletons that easily absorb water.

5. Sponges attach themselves to the (bottom, surface) or to rocks.

6. Sponges grow in (one shape, many different shapes).

Part A

Write the name of the water animal that best matches each description. Choose from the names below.

clam	invertebrate	octopus	snail
coral animal	jellyfish	crustacean	sponge
crab	lobster	sea anemone	starfish

1. It is a group of water animals that has shells. _____.

2. It is a mollusk with a one-part shell. _____

3. It has a foot, which is a muscle under its body. _____

4. It is a mollusk that has eight arms. _____

5. It can stick out its stomach into an open clamshell. _____

6. It is a crustacean that usually moves sideways. _____

7. It has eyes on stems that stick out from its head. _____

8. It is a coelenterate that looks like a flower. _____

9. It is a coelenterate that has a skeleton. _____

10. It has a body that is filled with jellylike material. _____

11. It is an animal that can be used for cleaning. _____

Part B

Read each sentence. Write <u>True</u> if the sentence is true. Write <u>False</u> if the sentence is false.

1. Invertebrates are animals with backbones. _____

2. Coral colonies can grow together to make a coral reef. _____

3. A clam has a ligament that can close the two parts of its shell.

    _____

4. Lobsters molt, but crabs do not molt. _____

EXPLORE & DISCOVER

Make Ocean Environment Invertebrates

You Need

- a partner
- paints and markers
- string or yarn
- encyclopedia or books on ocean animals

- white paper
- glue or clear tape
- scissors

1. Start with the underwater ocean world you made in Unit 2. Add some invertebrate water animals to it.

2. Use books on ocean animals to find out which invertebrates are found in your ocean environment. The list on this page will help.

3. Work with your partner to choose the animals you will make. Use paper, markers, and paint to draw and paint your animals.

4. Cut out the animal shapes. Attach string or yarn for tentacles.

5. Use tape or glue to attach your animals to your underwater background. Create a realistic environment by planning your display.

Invertebrate Ocean Animals
sponges
corals
sea urchins
sea anemones
starfish
clams
oysters
sea snails
jellyfish
squid
octopuses
nautiluses
shrimp
crabs
lobsters

Write the Answer

Explain two ways that water invertebrates move.

_____

_____

_____

Fill in the circle in front of the word or phrase that best completes each sentence. The first one is done for you.

1. Starfish move with their
   - ● tube feet.
   - ⓑ jointed legs.
   - ⓒ stiff spines.

2. A sea anemone can sting tiny fish with its
   - ⓐ gills.
   - ⓑ sponges.
   - ⓒ tentacles.

3. Two kinds of coelenterates are
   - ⓐ crabs and lobsters.
   - ⓑ coral animals and jellyfish.
   - ⓒ clams and octopuses.

4. The largest group of invertebrates is the
   - ⓐ crustaceans.
   - ⓑ coelenterates.
   - ⓒ mollusks.

5. Losing a shell and growing a larger one is
   - ⓐ making a reef.
   - ⓑ a way of hiding.
   - ⓒ called molting.

6. New coral animals attach themselves to
   - ⓐ vertebrae.
   - ⓑ skeletons.
   - ⓒ plants.

Fill in the missing words.

7. Most mollusks have _____. (claws, shells)

8. A crab is a _____. (crustacean, coelenterate)

9. Lobsters have _____. (claws, scales)

Write the answer on the lines.

10. What is an invertebrate?

_____

_____

_____

What Is a Fish?

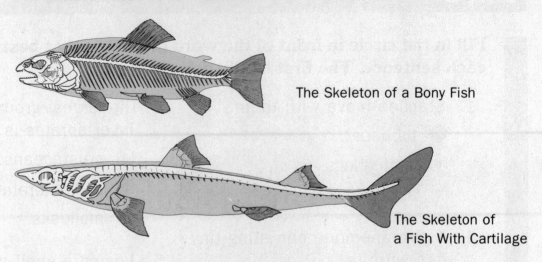

The Skeleton of a Bony Fish

The Skeleton of
a Fish With Cartilage

Fish are vertebrates, or animals with backbones. They live in fresh water or salt water. Most fish are **cold-blooded.** Their body temperature changes with the temperature of the water around them.

There are more than 20,000 different kinds of fish. Some fish have skeletons made of hard bone. Others have skeletons made of **cartilage,** which is softer than bone. A third group have mouths but no jaws. Fish can be almost any color, shape, or size. They can be as small as the $\frac{1}{2}$-inch dwarf goby or as big as the 50-foot whale shark. Some fish, such as skates, are as flat as a pancake. Others, such as eels, are long and thin like snakes.

Most fish have a head, a body, and a tail. They also have **fins.** Fins are found along the back, stomach, and sides of a fish. Fish use their fins to swim and to keep balanced. Most fish are covered with **scales,** or thin plates.

Fish have gills. They use their gills to get oxygen from water, like people use their lungs to get oxygen from air.

Some fish give birth to live young, but most lay eggs. In some fish, eggs hatch inside the parent's body. When fish are born, they may swim along with adult fish in a group called a **school.** Schools may have millions of fish in them.

A. Answer True or False.

1. There are over 20,000 different kinds of fish. _____

2. Some fish have skeletons made of hard bone. _____

3. Fish are vertebrate animals that live in fresh water and salt water.

   _____

4. Fish use their lungs to get oxygen from the air. _____

5. Most fish lay eggs. _____

6. A fish's body temperature always stays the same. _____

7. Some fish have mouths but no jaws. _____

B. Underline the correct words.

1. Fish use their (gills, fins) to get oxygen.

2. Most fish get oxygen from (air, water).

3. Most fish are (warm-blooded, cold-blooded).

4. Fish are (vertebrates, invertebrates).

5. Most fish are covered with (hair, scales).

6. Some fish have skeletons made of cartilage, which is (harder, softer) than bone.

7. Most fish have a head, a body, and a (foot, tail).

C. Use each word to write a sentence about fish.

1. fins _____

   _____

2. schools _____

   _____

3. scales _____

   _____

Eels

A Moray Eel

Eels are fish that are shaped like a snake. There are giant eels that grow to be 10 feet long. But most eels are about 3 feet long. Eels have slimy bodies that may be covered with scales. Eels do not have fins along the sides of their bodies, like most fish. They wriggle through the water like a water snake.

Most eels, like the moray eel, make their homes in the ocean near coral reefs. Moray eels have long, needlelike teeth. They curl up in holes in reefs during the day. At night, they surprise fish that swim by their holes and catch them in their teeth.

Some eels live in fresh water part of their lives and salt water part of their lives. Only a few fish can live in both environments. American eels are born in the ocean. When the young eels hatch from the eggs, they are tiny and clear like glass. After a few years, the eels swim to freshwater rivers and streams in North and Central America. These young eels are called elvers.

After 5 or 6 more years, the eels are fully grown. Then they swim back to the ocean to lay eggs. After they lay eggs, the eels die. The young eels hatch and swim in the ocean for 1 to 3 years. Then they swim to the same freshwater area where their parents lived.

A. Use the words below to complete the sentences.

clear	elvers	scales
eels	fins	snake
eggs		

1. Eels are fish that are shaped like a _____ .

2. Young eels that swim to freshwater rivers and streams are _____ .

3. Most _____ make their homes near coral reefs.

4. American eels are born in the ocean. When they hatch, they are tiny and _____ like glass.

5. Eels have slimy bodies that may be covered with _____ .

6. Eels lay _____ .

7. Eels do not have _____ on the sides of their bodies, like most fish.

B. Answer True or False.

1. Most eels are 12 feet long. _____

2. Moray eels have long, needlelike teeth. _____

3. Eels have many fins along the sides of their bodies. _____

4. Some eels live in fresh water part of their lives and salt water part of their lives. _____

5. When young eels hatch from eggs, they are dark brown. _____

6. Eels wriggle through the water like a water snake. _____

7. American eels are born in the ocean. _____

8. When American eels are fully grown, they swim back to the ocean to lay eggs. _____

Goldfish

Lionhead Goldfish

Calico Carp

Goldfish are a kind of freshwater fish called carp. They have been bred for their beauty. In the wild, many carp are a dull olive green color. Some carp may grow to be 40 inches long and may live to be 15 years old.

Sometimes an olive green carp gives birth to goldfish. Many years ago, breeders in China noticed that when goldfish mated, they always gave birth to gold babies. The breeders began to keep goldfish in bowls or ponds. They fed the fish special foods and tried to develop fancy fins and fancy colors. Some of the fish lived to be 50 years old.

There are many types of goldfish. Goldfish range from 2 to more than 12 inches long. They may be golden, red, red-gold, orange, brown, gray, or black. Some have spots of purple or lavender. Many have double winglike fins. A few goldfish have fringe around their heads.

Goldfish need little care, and most will live about 5 years. Natural food for goldfish includes worms, fleas, or plants. Breeders developed special diets for the fish so they would stay healthy and remain beautiful. Today, goldfish food can be bought at pet stores. It provides the best diet for goldfish kept as pets.

Goldfish live best in water that is about 65°F. The fish should be kept in a large container so they have enough room and can get enough air. Because goldfish have no eyelids, they need shade in the container.

A. Answer True or False.

1. Goldfish are carp that have been bred for their beauty. _____

2. Sometimes an olive green carp gives birth to silver babies. _____

3. There are 5,000 types of goldfish. _____

4. Goldfish need a lot of care. _____

5. Goldfish food provides the best diet for goldfish kept as pets. _____

6. Goldfish live best in water that is about 65°F. _____

7. Most goldfish live about 5 years. _____

B. Fill in the missing words.

1. Carp may grow to be _____ long and may live to be 15 years old. (40 inches, 40 feet)

2. Goldfish always give birth to _____ babies. (green, gold)

3. Breeders tried to develop goldfish with fancy fins and fancy _____. (eyes, colors)

4. Goldfish may be red, red-gold, orange, brown, gray, or _____. (black, blue)

5. Goldfish need a _____ container so they have enough room and can get enough air. (large, small)

6. Goldfish need shade because they have no _____. (fins, eyelids)

C. Draw lines to match each term with its description.

1. breeders   natural food for goldfish

2. carp   keep goldfish healthy and beautiful

3. worms   began to sell goldfish

4. special diets   a dull olive green freshwater fish

Bass

A Largemouth Black Bass

Bass are a group of fish that have long bodies with many bones. Some bass live in the ocean, and some live in freshwater lakes and streams.

Freshwater bass swim freely in lakes, ponds, and streams. They are big and strong. This makes freshwater bass popular for both sport fishing and for food. Freshwater bass are also fierce hunters. They have very few enemies.

The largemouth bass lives in the quiet waters of freshwater lakes. Most largemouth bass weigh about 4 pounds. Some grow to more than 2 feet long and can weigh 20 pounds.

Smallmouth bass live in large lakes and cold streams. They are very strong fighters for their size. Smallmouth bass can grow to be 1 foot long and weigh as much as 10 pounds.

All bass are **carnivores.** This means that they eat only meat. Freshwater bass hunt for fish, frogs, crayfish, and insects. Largemouth bass will even eat baby ducks.

More than 370 kinds of bass live in the ocean. The striped bass is a common saltwater fish found in the Atlantic Ocean. Saltwater bass are larger than freshwater bass. Groupers are a kind of bass that live in warm tropical waters. They can grow to be 8 feet long and may weigh over 500 pounds.

A. Use the words below to complete the sentences.

bass	foot	pounds
bodies	lakes	streams
carnivores	ocean	weigh

1. Bass are a group of fish that have long _____ with many bones.

2. Freshwater _____ are fierce hunters.

3. The largemouth bass lives in the quiet waters of freshwater _____.

4. Smallmouth bass live in large lakes and cold _____.

5. Smallmouth bass can grow to be 1 _____ long.

6. Largemouth bass can weigh 20 _____.

7. All bass are _____. They eat only meat.

8. More than 370 kinds of bass live in the _____.

9. Groupers are a kind of bass that can grow to be 8 feet long and may _____ over 500 pounds.

B. Write the letter for the correct answer.

1. Freshwater bass are fierce hunters. They have very few _____.
   (a) eggs   (b) enemies   (c) friends

2. Freshwater bass hunt for fish, frogs, crayfish, and _____.
   (a) cats   (b) people   (c) insects

3. All bass are carnivores. This means that they eat only _____.
   (a) meat   (b) plants   (c) when they are hungry

4. Groupers are a kind of bass that live in _____ tropical waters.
   (a) cold   (b) warm   (c) deep

5. The striped bass is a common saltwater fish found in _____.
   (a) ponds   (b) lakes   (c) the Atlantic Ocean

Sharks

A Shark

Sharks are fast-swimming fish that glide through water at speeds up to 40 miles an hour. Their graceful bodies are built for constant swimming and speed. Sharks' skeletons are made of cartilage.

A shark's eyes are on the side of its head, and its mouth is on its underside. A shark's body is covered with sharp, toothlike scales. Shark skin is so rough that it can be used just like sandpaper.

Most fish have a swim bladder. This is an organ that helps them float. Sharks do not have a swim bladder. Instead, they have large livers. The oil in their livers is lighter than water. This helps sharks float.

Different sharks have different kinds of teeth. Sharks that eat fish have sharp, triangular teeth to catch and hold their slippery prey. Sharks that eat shellfish have broad, flat teeth to crush shells. Some sharks have bristles to filter out plankton, or tiny ocean plants and animals. Sharks have several rows of teeth. New teeth replace the old teeth every few weeks.

Behind the mouth are gill slits. When sharks swim, water is forced out the gill slits. Most sharks must swim all the time so they can use their gills to breathe. Sharks use their fins for steering and balance as they swim. Their tail and back fin push them through the water.

A. Answer True or False.

1. Sharks are fast-swimming fish. _____

2. A shark's body is covered with smooth scales. _____

3. Different sharks have different kinds of teeth. _____

4. When sharks swim, water is forced out the gill slits. _____

5. Sharks glide through water at speeds up to 300 miles an hour.

   _____

6. The oil in sharks' livers helps them float. _____

7. Like most fish, sharks have a swim bladder. _____

B. Fill in the missing words.

1. Sharks' bodies are built for constant _____ and speed. (floating, swimming)

2. Shark skin is so _____ that it can be used just like sandpaper. (rough, smooth)

3. Most sharks must swim all the time so they can use their gills to

   _____. (eat, breathe)

4. Sharks use their _____ for steering and balance as they swim. (teeth, fins)

5. Sharks get new teeth to replace the old teeth every

   _____. (year, few weeks)

C. Draw lines to match each term with its description.

1. eyes   on the side of a shark's head

2. triangular teeth   crush shells

3. broad, flat teeth   filter plankton

4. bristles   hold slippery prey

5. rough scales   on the underside of a shark's head

6. mouth   cover a shark's body

Types of Sharks

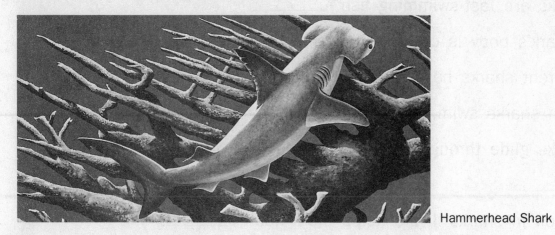
Hammerhead Shark

There are many types of sharks. Many sharks are fairly large, such as the great hammerhead and great white, which are 15 to 20 feet long. The largest shark is the whale shark, which averages 40 feet long. The smallest shark is the pygmy dogfish, which is only 5 or 6 inches long.

Some sharks are very dangerous. The great white shark is probably the best-known and most dangerous shark. It lives in cool temperate and tropical waters. Great white sharks are feared because they have attacked people many times.

The whale shark and the basking shark are not dangerous to people. These large sharks do not even eat other fish. They eat tiny ocean plants and animals called plankton. The basking shark floats on the surface as if it is basking in the sun.

The hammerhead shark is an unusual shark. Its head is T-shaped, like the head of a hammer. Its eyes are on each end of the crossbar of the T. Hammerheads are found in tropical oceans. They sometimes travel in schools.

Dogfish are small sharks that live in temperate or tropical seas. Unlike the great white shark, which gives birth to live young, the dogfish lays eggs. The eggs are in cases that cling to seaweed until they hatch. Like most other fish, young sharks can take care of themselves from birth.

A. Answer True or False.

1. The great white shark is the best-known and most dangerous shark. _____

2. The smallest shark is the whale shark. _____

3. The whale shark and the basking shark are not dangerous to people. _____

4. Hammerhead sharks are unusual because of their tails. _____

5. Dogfish are small sharks that live in temperate or tropical seas. _____

B. Draw lines to match each kind of shark with its description.

1. whale shark   floats on surface and eats plankton

2. basking shark   the largest shark

3. dogfish   small shark that lays eggs

4. great white   sometimes travel in schools

5. hammerhead   may attack people

C. Write the letter for the correct answer.

1. Hammerheads and _____ grow to be 15 to 20 feet long.
    (a) whale sharks   (b) dogfish   (c) great white sharks

2. The whale shark and the _____ eat plankton.
    (a) great white shark   (b) dogfish   (c) basking shark

3. The smallest shark is the pygmy _____, which is 5 or 6 inches long.
    (a) dogfish   (b) whale shark   (c) basking shark

4. Hammerheads have _____ heads.
    (a) T-shaped   (b) L-shaped   (c) pointed

5. The dogfish lays eggs in cases that cling to _____ until they hatch.
    (a) their mother   (b) seaweed   (c) other fish

Tuna

A School of Tuna

A tuna is a large, fast-swimming bony fish. Some tuna, such as the northern bluefin, grow to be 14 feet long and weigh over 750 pounds. But most tuna, such as the yellowfin, weigh less than 500 pounds. The frigate is a kind of tuna that never grows to be more than 2 feet long. It weighs about 10 pounds.

Tuna have dark blue backs and white stomachs. Different kinds of tuna have different-colored fins. Their streamlined bodies help them move through water easily. Tuna cannot pump water over their gills, so they must swim all the time. They speed along with their mouths open in order to breathe. Tuna can swim up to 50 miles an hour by moving their forked tails.

Most tuna are found in tropical salt water. They swim in large schools in the open ocean. Tuna use their great speed to catch other fish, such as mackerel. Some schools **migrate,** or travel, to colder waters during the summer. Then they migrate back to warmer waters in the fall.

Many people eat tuna. Tuna are easy to catch because they live in large groups. Schools of tuna are found easily by fishing boats because porpoises often swim above them. People catch tuna with nets or hooks and lines. A single boat can catch more than 200,000 pounds of tuna in a single day.

A. Answer True or False.

1. A tuna is a large, fast-swimming bony fish. _____

2. Different kinds of tuna have different-colored fins. _____

3. Most tuna are found in tropical fresh water. _____

4. Many people eat tuna. _____

B. Write the letter for the correct answer.

1. Tuna cannot pump water over their _____ , so they must swim all the time.
   (a) gills   (b) backs   (c) fins

2. Tuna swim in large _____ .
   (a) ponds   (b) schools   (c) lakes

3. Some schools migrate to _____ during the summer.
   (a) colder waters   (b) salt water   (c) fresh water

4. Tuna can swim up to _____ miles an hour by moving their forked tails.
   (a) 5   (b) 50   (c) 500

5. Tuna catch other fish, such as _____ .
   (a) sharks   (b) whales   (c) mackerel

6. A single boat can catch more than _____ of tuna in a single day.
   (a) 2 pounds   (b) 200 pounds   (c) 200,000 pounds

7. Schools of tuna are found easily by _____ .
   (a) fishing boats   (b) sharks   (c) mackerel

8. Tuna are _____ to catch because they live in large groups.
   (a) hard   (b) easy   (c) impossible

C. Draw lines to match each kind of tuna with its description.

1. northern bluefin   2 feet long and weighs 10 pounds

2. yellowfin   weighs less than 500 pounds

3. frigate   14 feet long and weighs over 750 pounds

Clownfish

The clownfish is never far from the sea anemone.

Clownfish are small, colorful saltwater fish. They are bright orange with black and white stripes. Clownfish are found in the warm tropical waters of the Pacific Ocean near coral reefs.

Adult clownfish live among sea anemones. A sea anemone is an animal that looks like a plant. It has many long tentacles sticking out around its mouth. Each tentacle has special cells that can sting and kill fish. The sea anemone uses the fish for food.

But sea anemones rarely try to kill the clownfish that live among them. Clownfish drop scraps of food and attract other fish that sea anemones eat. The sea anemone cleans fungus and other growths off the clownfish. It protects the clownfish from bigger fish. Both animals benefit from this relationship.

Clownfish are always within a few feet of the sea anemone. The female clownfish lays her eggs at the base of the sea anemone. Then the smaller male fans the eggs with his fins so they get enough air. When the eggs hatch, the young clownfish must make a home in another sea anemone. If they cannot find a new sea anemone, they are quickly caught and eaten by bigger fish.

A. **Use the words below to complete the sentences.**

anemones	eggs	stripes
coral reefs	fungus	tentacles

1. Clownfish are bright orange with black and white _____ .

2. Clownfish are found in warm tropical waters near

   _____ .

3. Adult clownfish live among sea _____ .

4. A sea anemone has many long _____ sticking out around its mouth.

5. The sea anemone cleans _____ and other growths off clownfish.

6. The female clownfish lays her _____ at the base of the sea anemone.

B. **Write the letter for the correct answer.**

1. Each tentacle of a sea anemone has special cells that can

   _____ other fish.
   (a) feed   (b) sting and kill   (c) catch

2. Sea anemones _____ try to kill the clownfish that live among them.
   (a) rarely   (b) often   (c) never

3. The sea anemone protects the clownfish from _____ .
   (a) crabs   (b) bigger fish   (c) squid

4. The male clownfish fans the _____ with his fins so they get enough air.
   (a) bigger fish   (b) squid   (c) eggs

5. Young clownfish must find room in a new _____ .
   (a) reef   (b) sea anemone   (c) fish

6. The sea anemone uses _____ for food.
   (a) fish   (b) plants   (c) coral

Sea Horses

The male sea horse carries eggs in his pouch until they hatch.

Sea horses are S-shaped fish that are about 5 inches long. Their bodies are covered with bony, bumpy plates. They are called sea horses because their heads are shaped like little horse heads. They can be many colors, but most are brown.

Sea horses are different from other fish in many ways. They swim forward in an upright position by moving their fins quickly. But sea horses spend most of their time floating with the current.

Sea horses have long snouts. They use their snouts to suck up plankton from the water. Sea horses can move one eye without moving the other. So they can see in several directions at the same time. With their tails, sea horses can hold on to seaweed and stay in one spot.

Sea horses have pouches on the underside of their bodies. When they reproduce, the female lays about 200 eggs in the male's pouch. Then the male sea horse carries the eggs until they hatch. When the young sea horses hatch, they are less than $\frac{1}{2}$ inch long. They drift and float until they can grasp seaweed or coral with their tails.

Underline the correct words.

1. Sea horses are S-shaped (fish, plankton).

2. Sea horses spend most of their time (swimming, floating).

3. Sea horses use their long snouts to (breathe, suck up plankton).

4. The female lays about 200 eggs in the male's (fins, pouch).

5. Sea horses grasp seaweed with their (fins, tails).

Manta Rays

A Manta Ray

The manta ray is a giant member of a group of fish called rays or skates. Like sharks, rays have skeletons made of cartilage instead of bone. Rays have wide, flat bodies with winglike fins. Their eyes are on the top side of their heads, and their mouth and gill slits are on the underside. They have long, narrow tails.

Smaller rays, including the stingray, live on the bottom of the ocean. Their flat bodies make them hard to see. They have heavy, round teeth that can crush the shells of snails and clams.

Manta rays live near the surface. They can grow to be over 20 feet across and may weigh 3,000 pounds. They swim by moving their long side fins up and down. This slow, lazy motion makes manta rays look as if they are flying underwater.

Manta rays eat plankton, or small ocean organisms. They use two flaps of skin next to their mouths to scoop up food. Then they catch plankton in a strainer as water passes over their gills.

Answer True or False.

1. The manta ray is a small member of a group of fish called rays and skates. _____

2. The stingray lives on the surface of the ocean. _____

3. Manta rays eat plankton. _____

Deep-Sea Fish

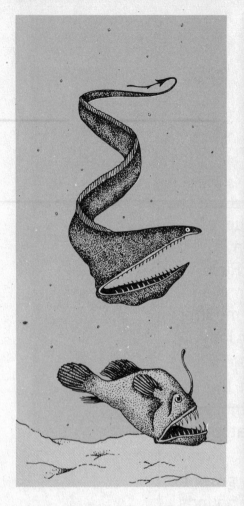

A Gulper Eel and an Angler Fish

The deep parts of the ocean are very different from the surface areas. Below 600 feet, there is only dim light. Below 3,000 feet, there is almost no light. The water is very cold. Bottom dwellers live under great pressure from all the water pushing down on them. Fish that dwell at the bottom of the ocean have special features to help them live.

Because little light reaches their home, some fish, such as the lantern fish, have glands that give off light. They use their lights to see where they are going and to attract other fish.

One of the strangest of the deep-sea fish is the gulper eel. Some gulper eels have lights on the end of their tails to attract fish they like to eat. The gulper eel has a huge mouth and a stomach that stretches. It can eat fish that are bigger than it is!

Instead of gliding near the surface of the ocean like a tuna or a shark, the angler fish sits on the bottom. It has a long piece of skin that dangles in front of its mouth. This piece of skin looks like a worm. When fish come near and try to eat it, the angler catches its meal.

Underline the correct words.

1. Below 3,000 feet, there is almost no (life, light).

2. Bottom dwellers live under great (light, pressure).

3. The water is very (hot, cold) at the bottom of the ocean.

4. Fish that dwell at the bottom have special (bones, features).

Part A

Read each sentence. Write <u>True</u> if the sentence is true. Write <u>False</u> if the sentence is false.

1. Eels are not fish. _____

2. Fish are cold-blooded vertebrates. _____

3. Great white sharks are not dangerous. _____

4. Goldfish are a kind of freshwater fish called carp. _____

5. Like sharks, manta rays have skeletons made of cartilage. _____

6. Clownfish have tentacles that sting other fish. _____

7. The female sea horse lays eggs in the male's pouch. _____

8. Some bass live in the ocean and some live in fresh water. _____

9. Some eels can live in fresh water and salt water. _____

Part B

Fill in the missing words.

1. The _____ fish has a piece of skin that dangles in front of its mouth and attracts other fish. (angler, shark)

2. Adult clownfish live near sea _____ for protection. (snakes, anemones)

3. Fish use their _____ to get oxygen. (fins, gills)

4. The _____ is a kind of bass that lives in the ocean and may weigh 500 pounds. (largemouth, grouper)

5. Different kinds of sharks have different kinds of _____. (teeth, fins)

6. Seahorses are S-shaped _____. (birds, fish)

7. Tuna swim _____. (alone, in schools)

8. The body of a manta ray is wide and _____. (flat, round)

9. Tuna have dark blue backs and white _____. (stomachs, fins)

Make a Fish Reference Book

You Need

- 1 sheet of poster paper
- colored pencils
- books on fish or encyclopedia

1. Study a fish that interests you or has an unusual adaptation. Use books on fish or use encyclopedias to find pictures and information on the fish.

2. On a large sheet of poster paper make a detailed drawing of the fish in its environment. Color the fish accurately, using colored pencils.

3. Record interesting facts about the fish on the poster paper. Answer the questions.

4. What is the name of your fish? Where does it live? What does it look like and how long is it? What does it eat and how does it get its food? What are some interesting facts about it?

5. Attach your fish card to others from your class to make a fish reference book.

Swordfish

The swordfish lives in salt water.

The swordfish lives in all warm seas.

The swordfish has a long upper jaw that looks like a sword.

The swordfish eats squid and most fish that travel in schools.

Write the Answer

Do you think your fish could survive in the ocean environment you created in Units 1 through 3? Explain your answer.

_____

_____

_____

Fill in the circle in front of the word or phrase that best completes each sentence. The first one is done for you.

1. A fish that lives in both fresh water and salt water is the
   - ● eel.
   - ⓑ goldfish.
   - ⓒ whale shark.

2. One fish that has cartilage instead of bone is the
   - ⓐ clownfish.
   - ⓑ shark.
   - ⓒ goldfish.

3. To help them live, deep-sea fish have special
   - ⓐ features.
   - ⓑ eggs.
   - ⓒ bones.

4. One fish that is dangerous to people is the
   - ⓐ manta ray.
   - ⓑ great white shark.
   - ⓒ clownfish.

5. A sea horse keeps its eggs in a
   - ⓐ nest.
   - ⓑ case.
   - ⓒ pouch.

6. A name for one kind of bass is
   - ⓐ largemouth.
   - ⓑ hammerhead.
   - ⓒ gulper.

Fill in the missing words.

7. Tuna, dogfish, and rays are all _____. (fish, sharks)

8. Clownfish live near sea _____. (reefs, anemones)

9. Goldfish need little _____. (air, care)

Write the answer on the lines.

10. List four of the body parts that most fish have.

_____

_____

_____

UNIT 5
Water Reptiles

What Is a Reptile?

Alligator

Reptiles are vertebrates, or animals with backbones. Most reptiles live on land, but some live in water. Other reptiles can live both on land and in water.

All reptiles have lungs. They get the oxygen they need by breathing air. Water reptiles can stay underwater for long periods of time. But they must swim to the surface to fill their lungs with air.

Reptiles are cold-blooded. The body temperature of cold-blooded animals changes with the temperature of the air or water around them. For this reason, reptiles cannot live in the coldest places on Earth. Their body temperature would get too cold. Reptiles can be found living in warm and hot climates throughout the world.

Reptiles' bodies are covered with dry scales or hard plates. Most reptiles have low, long bodies, with long tails and four short legs. Snakes are reptiles that do not have legs. Most reptiles reproduce by laying eggs on land. A few reptiles give birth to live young.

In this unit, you will read about water reptiles, such as alligators and turtles. Water reptiles spend at least part of their lives in water.

A. Fill in the missing words.

1. Reptiles are _____ . (vertebrates, invertebrates)

2. Reptiles are animals _____ backbones. (without, with)

3. All reptiles have _____ . (gills, lungs)

4. Reptiles are _____ . (cold-blooded, warm-blooded)

5. Reptiles' bodies are often covered with dry _____ .
   (scales, hair)

6. Nearly all reptiles reproduce by _____
   on land. (giving birth to live young, laying eggs)

B. Answer True or False.

1. Most reptiles have short bodies with short tails and two long legs.

   _____

2. Reptiles can live in the coldest places on Earth. _____

3. Some reptiles can live both on land and in water. _____

4. Snakes are not reptiles because they do not have legs. _____

5. A few reptiles give birth to live young. _____

C. Answer the questions.

1. What are the bodies of reptiles like? _____

   _____

   _____

   _____

2. Why do reptiles not live in the coldest places on Earth? _____

   _____

3. If water reptiles stay underwater for a long time, how do they breathe?

   _____

   _____

Sea Snakes

Sea Snake

Sea snakes are reptiles. They live only in the warm waters of the Pacific and Indian oceans. They live in shallow water. There are about 50 different kinds. Most are from 4 to 10 feet long. Some have bodies that get wider toward the tail. Some have tails that look like paddles. These features help them swim. Most sea snakes are dull green or light brown. Some have yellow bellies.

All sea snakes are **poisonous.** Their **venom,** or poison, is very strong. Sea snakes kill small fish with venom from their fangs. Sea snakes do not usually attack people. Sometimes sea snakes get caught in fishermen's nets. They may bite when being freed from the nets.

Most kinds of sea snakes give birth to live young. The young are born at sea. A few kinds of sea snakes lay eggs. These snakes leave the water when they are going to lay eggs. They usually lay their eggs on coral reefs.

Like other water reptiles, sea snakes have lungs, not gills. But the nostrils and lungs of sea snakes are different from those of other water animals. With their nostrils and lungs, sea snakes can take some oxygen directly out of the water. Sea snakes can stay underwater for up to 8 hours.

A. Use the words below to complete the sentences.

A few	Most	reptiles
invertebrates	poisonous	sea snakes

1. Sea snakes are _____ that live only in the warm waters of the Pacific and Indian oceans.

2. Some _____ have bodies that get wider toward the tail.

3. All sea snakes are _____ .

4. _____ kinds of sea snakes give birth to live young.

5. _____ kinds of sea snakes lay eggs.

B. Answer True or False.

1. Sea snakes have lungs, not gills. _____

2. Almost all kinds of sea snakes spend their whole lives on land.

_____

3. Sea snakes usually attack people. _____

4. Some sea snakes have tails that look like paddles.

_____

5. A few kinds of sea snakes lay their eggs on coral reefs. _____

6. Sea snakes can stay underwater for less than 2 minutes.

_____

C. Use each word to write a sentence about sea snakes.

1. nostrils _____

_____

2. venom _____

_____

Freshwater Snakes

The northern water snake is a freshwater snake that is not poisonous.

Some kinds of snakes can be found in the fresh waters of lakes, rivers, and streams. These freshwater snakes go into water to hide from enemies and to catch fish to eat. But most of them come out of the water often. They spend much of their time on the branches of trees near the water, warming themselves in the sun.

Most freshwater snakes look similar to land snakes. Some freshwater snakes will bite if they are angered or afraid. The bite of most freshwater snakes is **nonpoisonous,** or has no poison. But bites from any animal can lead to an infection.

One kind of freshwater snake is the northern water snake. Its body has red-brown bands or spots on a yellow background. Like other freshwater snakes, the northern water snake gives birth to live young in the water. Right after they are born, the young snakes do not get any care from their parents. Most young reptiles can take care of themselves as soon as they are born.

A. **Answer <u>True</u> or <u>False</u>.**

1. Some kinds of snakes can be found in fresh water. _____

2. The bite of some freshwater snakes is nonpoisonous. _____

3. The northern water snake lays eggs. _____

B. **Answer the question.**

What do freshwater snakes do when they come out of the water? _____

_____

_____

Cottonmouths

Cottonmouth Snake on Land and in Water

The cottonmouth is a very poisonous snake that lives in the southern United States. Cottonmouths are found around swamps, marshes, and other wet places. For this reason, cottonmouths are thought of as freshwater snakes. They are also known as water moccasins.

A cottonmouth has long, sharp teeth called **fangs.** When a cottonmouth bites, venom goes through its fangs. A cottonmouth feeds on frogs, fish, and other vertebrates. A bite from a cottonmouth is dangerous. It can kill a person.

The young of cottonmouths are born live. They are reddish brown, with brown bands with white edges. As they grow older, cottonmouths become dark olive or brown. The average length of cottonmouths is from 3 to 4 feet, although some can grow to be 6 feet long.

Underline the correct words.

1. The cottonmouth is a snake that lives in the (northern, southern) United States.

2. When a cottonmouth (sleeps, bites), venom goes through its fangs.

3. The young of cottonmouths (are born live, hatch from eggs).

4. Cottonmouths are also known as (sea snakes, water moccasins).

Crocodiles and Alligators

Which is the crocodile, and which is
the alligator? The teeth should tell you.

Crocodiles and alligators are reptiles that are alike in many ways. Both reptiles have long **snouts,** long tails, four short legs, tough skin, and sharp teeth. They both spend their time in water and on land.

Crocodiles live around swamps and riverbanks in warm places all over the world. In the United States, they can be found in fresh and salt water in southern Florida. Alligators can be found in the southern United States and in China. Crocodiles and alligators often float just below the surface of the water. They also lie on land, taking in the heat of the sun. They feed on fish, frogs, and other water animals. As they get older and bigger, they may eat birds and land animals.

Like other reptiles, crocodiles and alligators are cold-blooded. They both reproduce by laying eggs. But there are some differences between crocodiles and alligators. The usual length of an adult American crocodile is 12 feet. Alligators are slightly smaller. A crocodile's snout is more pointed than an alligator's snout. Some teeth of a crocodile can be seen when its mouth is closed. This is not true of an alligator. Alligators are not as fierce as crocodiles. Crocodiles will even attack people.

A. Fill in the missing words.

1. Crocodiles and alligators are reptiles that are _____.
   (alike, different)

2. Crocodiles and alligators spend their time _____.
   (only in water, in water and on land)

3. Crocodiles live in _____ places all over the world.
   (warm, cold)

4. Crocodiles and alligators are _____.
   (warm-blooded, cold-blooded)

5. There are _____ differences between crocodiles and alligators.
   (no, some)

6. Alligators are slightly _____ than crocodiles.
   (smaller, bigger)

B. Write crocodile, alligator, or both to answer the questions.

1. Which reptile has a long tail? _____

2. Which reptile has a more pointed snout? _____

3. Which reptile has sharp teeth? _____

4. Which reptile does not show its teeth when its mouth is closed?

   _____

5. Which reptile will attack people? _____

6. Which reptile lays eggs? _____

C. Answer True or False.

1. Crocodiles and alligators lie on land, taking in the heat of the sun.

   _____

2. Crocodiles and alligators feed on water animals and land animals.

   _____

3. Crocodiles have tough skin, but alligators do not. _____

4. Both reptiles like to rest on the ocean bottom. _____

Green Turtles

After sea turtles hatch, they move to the water, where they will spend the rest of their lives.

A turtle is the only reptile with a **shell.** The shell is made of hard plates and is usually round at the top and flat on the bottom. It almost completely covers the turtle. Only the head, legs, and tail stick out from the shell. Some kinds of turtles can pull their head, legs, and tail into their shell when they are in danger. Then they are safe from enemies.

One of the largest groups of turtles is the sea turtles. Like land turtles and other water turtles, sea turtles have hard shells. But sea turtles cannot pull their head, legs, and tail into their shell. For this reason, sea turtles cannot easily protect themselves. People often catch them and use the turtle meat for food.

There are several kinds of sea turtles. One kind is the green turtle. Green turtles can be found in the Caribbean Sea and in other warm waters. Green turtles can grow to be 4 feet long. They almost never leave the water. But they do go on land to lay their eggs. The female green turtle digs a hole in sand or soil for the eggs. After covering the eggs with sand, the female goes back to the water and never returns. When the young hatch, they scratch their way up to the surface. From then on, they take care of themselves.

People may be the worst enemy that green turtles have. People catch them and eat the turtle meat. They also find the eggs and eat them. About 25 years ago, the green turtle was in danger of dying out. Since then, however, steps have been taken to protect green turtles.

A. Write the letter for the correct answer.

1. The turtle is the only reptile with _____.
   (a) legs   (b) a shell   (c) a backbone

2. Sea turtles _____ pull their head, legs, and tail into their shell.
   (a) often   (b) cannot   (c) can

3. People eat turtle _____.
   (a) heads   (b) shells   (c) meat

4. One kind of sea turtle is the _____ turtle.
   (a) green   (b) black   (c) land

5. Green turtles go on land to _____.
   (a) rest   (b) get some sun   (c) lay their eggs

6. _____ may be the greatest enemy that green turtles have.
   (a) Water   (b) People   (c) Bigger turtles

B. Use the words below to complete the sentences.

| care | hatch | land |
| eggs | hole | water |

1. Green turtles go on _____ to lay their eggs.

2. The female green turtle digs a hole for the _____.

3. The female covers the eggs and goes back to the _____.

4. When the young _____, they scratch their way up to the surface.

5. From then on, the young turtles take _____ of themselves.

C. Answer the question.

What are two reasons why people may be the worst enemy that green

turtles have? _____

_____

Snapping Turtles

Common Snapping Turtle   Alligator Snapper

You can tell something about a snapping turtle just from its name. If you pick up a snapping turtle, it will snap and try to bite your hand. Snapping turtles are fierce reptiles. They have long necks that can move their heads quickly. They have powerful jaws that bite hard. Snapping turtles want to be left alone. If you bother them, watch out!

Snapping turtles are freshwater turtles. There are two kinds. The common snapping turtle, or snapper, can be found from central Canada to the northern part of South America. The alligator snapper lives in the southeastern United States. Both kinds spend most of their time underwater, in muddy ponds and shallow, slow-moving rivers. From time to time, they come up to the surface to breathe.

Snapping turtles are **omnivores,** which means they eat plants as well as animals. They feed on algae and other plants. They also eat fish and other water animals. The alligator snapper often lies underwater on the muddy bottom, with its jaws wide open. It has a tongue that wiggles and looks like a worm. Fish like to eat worms. A fish, thinking the tongue is a worm, will swim into the alligator snapper's mouth. The alligator snapper then snaps its jaws shut.

A. **Underline the correct words.**

1. If you pick up a snapping turtle, it will try to (run away, bite your hand).

2. Snapping turtles are (fierce, friendly) reptiles.

3. Snapping turtles want to be (bothered, left alone).

4. Snapping turtles are (saltwater, freshwater) turtles.

5. The two kinds of snapping turtles are the common snapping turtle and the (crocodile, alligator) snapper.

6. Snapping turtles spend most of their time (on land, underwater).

7. Snapping turtles eat (only animals, plants and animals).

B. **Answer <u>True</u> or <u>False</u>.**

1. Snapping turtles come up to the surface of the water to breathe. _____

2. Snapping turtles have powerful jaws. _____

3. Snapping turtles spend most of their time at the bottom of the ocean. _____

4. There are many different kinds of snapping turtles. _____

5. Snapping turtles are omnivores. _____

6. Snapping turtles can move their heads quickly. _____

7. An alligator snapper has a tongue that wiggles and looks like a worm. _____

C. **Use each word to write a sentence about snapping turtles.**

1. tongue _____

_____

2. jaws _____

_____

Marine Iguanas

Marine Iguana

Iguanas belong to a group of reptiles called lizards. Many different kinds of iguanas live on land. The marine iguana, however, is the only lizard that lives in the sea as well as on land. It is called a marine iguana because marine means "of the sea."

Marine iguanas are found only on the Galapagos Islands in the Pacific Ocean. They may look dangerous, but they are actually very peaceful. These gray-black lizards use their strong, sharp claws to climb the rocky shores of the Galapagos Islands. Marine iguanas are good swimmers. Their flat tails look like paddles. The tails help push them through the water.

Marine iguanas spend most of their time resting in the sun or shade of the rocky coast. They stay close to the sea at all times. They feed on algae and seaweed from the water.

Answer True or False.

1. The marine iguana is the only lizard that lives in the sea as well as on land. _____

2. Marine iguanas are poor swimmers. _____

3. Marine iguanas feed on algae and seaweed. _____

Part A

Use the words below to complete the sentences.

alligator	freshwater snake	reptiles
Cottonmouths	green turtle	sea snakes
Crocodiles	marine iguana	snapping turtle

1. Some _____ have bodies that get wider toward the tail.

2. The northern water snake is one kind of _____.

3. _____ are also known as water moccasins.

4. _____ are like alligators in many ways.

5. The _____ is one kind of sea turtle that cannot pull its head, legs, and tail into its shell.

6. If you pick up a _____, it will snap and try to bite your hand.

7. The _____ is the only lizard that lives in the sea as well as on land.

8. The teeth of an _____ cannot be seen when its mouth is closed.

Part B

Read each sentence. Write **True** if the sentence is true. Write **False** if the sentence is false.

1. Reptiles are vertebrates, or animals with backbones. _____

2. All reptiles live in the water. _____

3. Like other water reptiles, sea snakes have gills. _____

4. Snapping turtles are freshwater turtles. _____

5. A turtle is the only reptile with a shell. _____

EXPLORE & DISCOVER

Make a Marine Iguana

You Need

- 2 sheets of butcher paper
- newspaper
- masking tape
- stapler
- pipe cleaners
- strips of cardboard
- scissors
- paint

1. Look at the pictures of the marine iguana here and on page 86.

2. Sketch an outline of its body on two sheets of butcher paper. To allow for stuffing, make the outline 1 inch larger than it needs to be. Cut out the outline.

3. Draw on cardboard and cut out the iguana's pointy spines. Staple the spines between the cutouts from head to tail. Stuff the body and tail with crumpled newspapers as you staple it closed.

4. To make each pair of legs, roll sheets of newspaper into a tube. Put tape around each tube and then bend into a U shape. Tape the tubes to the body. Tape 5 pipe cleaners to each leg to form claws.

5. Cover your iguana with strips of papier-mâché. Allow to dry overnight. Paint when dry.

Write the Answer

Explain how the shape of the marine iguana's tail helps it swim.

_____

_____

Fill in the circle in front of the word or phrase that best completes each sentence. The first one is done for you.

1. A reptile with a long snout is the
   - ⓐ sea snake.
   - ● alligator.
   - ⓒ sea turtle.

2. A poisonous snake from the southern United States is the
   - ⓐ cottonmouth.
   - ⓑ northern water snake.
   - ⓒ iguana.

3. The only lizard that lives in the sea and on the land is the
   - ⓐ green turtle.
   - ⓑ marine iguana.
   - ⓒ sea snake.

4. The reptile with a tongue that looks like a worm is the
   - ⓐ alligator.
   - ⓑ cottonmouth.
   - ⓒ alligator snapper.

5. There are two kinds of
   - ⓐ snapping turtles.
   - ⓑ marine iguanas.
   - ⓒ northern water snakes.

6. The only reptile with a shell is the
   - ⓐ freshwater snake.
   - ⓑ iguana.
   - ⓒ turtle.

Fill in the missing words.

7. All reptiles have _____. (backbones, legs)

8. Reptiles are _____-blooded. (warm, cold)

9. All sea snakes are _____. (warm-blooded, poisonous)

Write the answer on the lines.

10. What are two ways in which reptiles reproduce?

   _____

   _____

   _____

UNIT 6
Water Birds

Loon

Grebe

What Is a Bird?

Birds are vertebrates, or animals with backbones. They are different from the other animals that you have learned about because birds are **warm-blooded.** The body temperature of warm-blooded animals always stays the same, even if the temperature around them changes.

Birds are the only animals that have **feathers.** Feathers help birds stay warm and dry. Birds have **wings.** Both wings and feathers help birds fly.

Not all birds can fly. Penguins are water birds that cannot fly. But they are excellent swimmers. A penguin's wings are shaped like flippers. They use these flippers and their webbed feet to swim through the water. Other water birds are great divers. The loon can dive down more than 150 feet under the water.

Most water birds live near lakes, ponds, and wetland areas. Many water birds swim to find food. But some wade or dive into the water to find their meals.

Some water birds live in large groups called **flocks.** Many flocks that live in the north migrate, or travel, to warmer areas in the south during the winter. They migrate south to find food. In the spring, they return to the north to reproduce.

Most water birds make **nests.** A nest may be made of twigs or mud. It may also be a hole in a tree or in the dirt. Grebes are water birds that make floating nests that are attached to water plants. All birds hatch from eggs. They stay in the nest until they can take care of themselves.

A. Answer True or False.

1. The body temperature of warm-blooded animals always changes. _____

2. Birds are the only animals that have feathers. _____

3. Feathers help birds stay warm and dry. _____

4. All birds can fly. _____

5. All water birds wade to find their meals. _____

B. Fill in the missing words.

1. Birds have _____. (backbones, shells)

2. Birds are _____ animals. (cold-blooded, warm-blooded)

3. Penguins are water birds that cannot _____. (swim, fly)

4. Some water birds are great _____. (climbers, divers)

5. Some water birds live in flocks that migrate to the _____ during the winter. (south, north)

6. Most water birds make _____. (boats, nests)

7. All birds _____. (hatch from eggs, give birth to live young)

8. Both wings and feathers help birds to _____. (swim, fly)

9. Most water birds live near lakes, ponds, and _____ areas. (wetland, desert)

C. Draw lines to match each term with its description.

1. flocks   can dive down 150 feet under the water

2. loons   cannot fly but are excellent swimmers

3. grebes   large groups of birds

4. penguins   make floating nests

Gulls

Gull in Flight

Gulls are long-winged birds. Their bodies may be 11 to 30 inches long. But a gull's **wing span,** or the length of its wings from one tip to the other, may be more than 5 feet long. Most adult gulls have light gray backs and white breasts. They may have black feathers on their wing tips. Most gulls have stocky bodies and square tails.

Gulls can drink salt water or fresh water. For this reason, gulls can live near any large body of water, such as an ocean or freshwater lake.

Gulls eat fish and other water animals. They will also eat insects, garbage, rotten meat, eggs, and the young of other birds. Because gulls eat any garbage or food that floats, they help keep the water clean. In Salt Lake City, Utah, the settlers made a monument to the great flocks of gulls that ate millions of grasshoppers and saved their crops.

Many gulls migrate south to warmer areas in the winter. In the spring, they return north to make nests of grass. They build their nests on rocky ledges or in marshes. The young gulls are covered with fluffy feathers called **down.** Down is very soft and thick. It helps the young gulls stay warm. The young gulls are cared for by their parents until they can fly.

A. Answer True or False.

1. Gulls are short-winged birds. _____

2. Gulls can drink salt water or fresh water. _____

3. Gulls can live near any large body of water. _____

4. Gulls will only eat other birds. _____

5. Gulls help keep the water clean. _____

6. Many gulls migrate south to warmer areas in the winter. _____

7. Most gulls have stocky bodies and square tails. _____

8. Gulls make nests of rocks. _____

B. Write the letter for the correct answer.

1. A gull's wing span may be more than _____ long.
   (a) 50 feet   (b) 5 feet   (c) 10 feet

2. Most adult gulls have light gray backs and white _____.
   (a) feet   (b) tails   (c) breasts

3. Gulls' bodies may be 11 to _____ long.
   (a) 300 inches   (b) 30 inches   (c) 30 feet

4. Gulls build their nests on rocky ledges or in _____.
   (a) marshes   (b) cities   (c) the woods

5. In Salt Lake City, Utah, settlers made a monument to gulls that ate

   millions of _____.
   (a) birds   (b) dead fish   (c) grasshoppers

6. Young gulls are covered with fluffy feathers called _____.
   (a) wing tips   (b) down   (c) tail feathers

7. In the spring, gulls return north to make nests of _____.
   (a) grass   (b) pebbles   (c) sticks

8. Young gulls are cared for by their parents until they can _____.
   (a) swim   (b) fly   (c) walk

9. Down helps the young gulls stay _____.
   (a) in the nest   (b) clean   (c) warm

Kingfishers

A Kingfisher

Kingfishers are colorful birds with bright blue or green heads and backs. Their breasts may be white with bands of green or blue. Many have **crests,** or feathers that stick up, on their heads. Kingfishers have large heads, short necks, and long, heavy, pointed **bills,** or beaks. Their bodies are 4 to 18 inches long with short tails, short legs, and tiny feet.

Kingfishers are found throughout the world, except in polar areas and some islands in the ocean. Some live in forests, but most live near water. Kingfishers are carnivores. They eat fish, crayfish, crabs, frogs, tadpoles, lizards, insects, small snakes, and turtles.

When hunting, a kingfisher may sit on a tree branch for hours watching the water below. When it sees a fish or other food, it dives down to catch it. It may spear the animal with its sharp bill or catch it in its mouth. The kingfisher then throws the animal in the air and swallows it headfirst. Sometimes a fish is too big to swallow in one gulp. So the kingfisher sits with the fish's tail sticking out of its mouth until the head is digested.

Kingfishers live alone except when they mate. Then a male and a female work together to dig a **burrow,** or tunnel, in the side of a riverbank. At the end of the burrow is a nesting place. It is big enough for the female bird to lay eggs. After the eggs hatch, the parents teach the young birds how to fish. Then the young can live on their own.

A. **Use the words below to complete the sentences.**

burrow	eggs	forest
crests	feathers	spear
dives	fish	water

1. Many kingfishers have _____, or feathers that stick up, on their heads.

2. When hunting, the kingfisher may sit on a branch for hours, watching the _____ below.

3. When a kingfisher sees a fish, it _____ down to catch it.

4. Kingfishers eat _____.

5. When kingfishers mate they dig a _____.

6. After the _____ hatch, the parents teach the young birds how to fish.

7. Kingfishers have bright blue or green _____ on their backs.

8. Some kingfishers live in the _____.

9. A kingfisher may _____ fish with its sharp bill.

B. **Answer True or False.**

1. Kingfishers are colorful birds. _____

2. Kingfishers have long, heavy, pointed bills. _____

3. Kingfishers are found in polar regions. _____

4. Most kingfishers live near water. _____

5. Kingfishers live in large groups called flocks. _____

6. Kingfishers eat crayfish, frogs, tadpoles, lizards, insects, and snakes. _____

7. The parents teach the young birds how to fish. _____

Flamingos

Flamingos

Flamingos are large pink water birds that are usually 3 to 5 feet tall. They have long, curved necks, tall legs that look like stilts, and webbed feet. Flamingos are found in tropical climates, where they live in large groups called colonies. They usually make a low sound. But when flamingos are threatened, they honk loudly like geese.

Most flamingos eat shellfish and algae. They wade in shallow water to find their food. When flamingos eat, they put their heads and curved bills, or beaks, in the water. They use their tongues to pump water through their bills. With the points along the edges of their bills, flamingos separate mud and water from food. Flamingos get their beautiful pink color from the shellfish they eat.

Adult flamingos make a large mound of mud to hold their eggs. The female usually lays one egg a year in a hole at the top of the mud nest. Fluffy white chicks hatch after about a month. Chicks are fed liquid from their parent's digestive system. The chicks turn pink as they get older. Chicks stay together in a group until they are about 3 months old. Then they can take care of themselves.

A. Answer True or False.

1. Flamingos are large pink water birds. _____

2. Flamingos only eat mud. _____

3. Adult flamingos make mounds of mud for nests. _____

4. Flamingos lay eggs. _____

5. When threatened, flamingos quack like ducks. _____

6. Chicks are fed from their parent's digestive system. _____

B. Write the letter for the correct answer.

1. Flamingos are usually _____ tall.
   (a) 50 feet   (b) 1 foot   (c) 3 to 5 feet

2. Flamingos _____ in shallow water to find their food.
   (a) wade   (b) dive   (c) swim

3. Chicks turn _____ as they get older.
   (a) pink   (b) blue   (c) green

4. Flamingos use their _____ to pump water through their bills.
   (a) feet   (b) wings   (c) tongues

5. Flamingos usually make a _____ sound.
   (a) high   (b) low   (c) loud

6. Flamingos live in _____ climates.
   (a) tropical   (b) polar   (c) temperate

7. Flamingo chicks hatch after about a _____.
   (a) year   (b) month   (c) day

C. Draw lines to match each term with its description.

1. chicks   large groups of flamingos

2. shellfish   stay together in a group for 3 months

3. bills   give flamingos their beautiful pink color

4. colonies   have points along the edges

97

Penguins

King Penguins

Adélie Penguins

Penguins are black-and-white water birds. They live in the southern half of the world where icy Antarctic currents flow. Penguins cannot fly, but they are good swimmers. They use their wings and webbed feet to swim and dive for the fish they eat.

Penguins have white breasts with black backs and heads. They may have a crest of feathers that sticks up on each side of their heads. Some penguins also have bright yellow feathers around their necks. Their waterproof feathers are short and thick to help protect them from the cold. Penguins also have a layer of fat under their skin that acts like a blanket to keep them warm.

Penguins stand up on short legs. The most common type of penguin is the adélie penguin. It is about $1\frac{1}{2}$ feet tall and weighs about 15 pounds.

Penguins raise their young in huge colonies, called **rookeries.** A rookery may have as many as one million birds. Adélie penguins build nests of pebbles. After spending the winter months in the ocean, adélie penguins return to their colony to lay eggs. They return to the same place year after year. Sometimes they walk over 200 miles of ice to find their old nests.

The female adélie penguin usually lays two eggs. Both parents stay in the colony until the eggs hatch. They do not eat or wash while they are waiting for the eggs to hatch. So the parents become thinner and dirtier. Once the chicks are hatched, the parents go to sea to feed.

A. **Use the words below to complete the sentences.**

adélie	eggs	fly
birds	fat	rookeries
chicks	feathers	southern

1. Penguins are black-and-white water _____.

2. Penguins live in the _____ half of the world.

3. Penguins' waterproof _____ are short and thick to help protect them from the cold.

4. Penguins have a layer of _____ under their skin that acts like a blanket to keep them warm.

5. The most common type of penguin is the _____ penguin.

6. Penguins raise their young in huge colonies called

   _____.

7. The female adélie lays two _____.

8. Once the _____ are hatched, the parents go to sea to feed.

9. Penguins cannot _____.

B. **Write the letter for the correct answer.**

1. Adélie penguins build nests of _____.
   (a) ice   (b) sticks   (c) pebbles

2. Sometimes adélie penguins _____ over 200 miles of ice to find their old nests.
   (a) swim   (b) fly   (c) walk

3. Parents do not eat or wash while they are waiting for the eggs to

   _____.

   (a) migrate   (b) hatch   (c) lay

4. Penguins are good _____.
   (a) swimmers   (b) flyers   (c) hunters

Puffins

Puffins

Puffins are small water birds found along northern seacoasts. They are sometimes called sea parrots because of their large, triangular beaks that are marked with bright colors. Puffins that live along the northern seacoasts of North America have big heads, thick necks, and stocky bodies. They have black backs and necks, whitish cheeks, and white breasts.

Puffins are expert swimmers and divers and spend most of their time at sea. They can dive from the air into the ocean. Then they use their wings and webbed feet to swim underwater and catch fish. Puffins can catch many small fish in their large beaks in a single dive.

During the summer, puffins come on land, where they live in large colonies on high rocks and cliffs. In North America, they can be found along the North Pacific and North Atlantic seacoasts.

During the mating season, or when they lay eggs, puffins' beaks turn bright red, yellow, and blue. They lay eggs in burrows, or tunnels, dug into grassy slopes near the shore. The male does most of the digging to make the burrow. The female puffin usually lays one egg in the burrow. After the egg hatches, the chick stays in the burrow for about 40 days. The parents bring the chick small fish to eat. Then the parents go back out to sea for the winter. The chick stays in the burrow for another week while its flight feathers grow. Then, at night, it flutters down to the water and learns to feed on its own.

A. Draw lines to match each term with its description.

1. sea parrots   turn bright red, yellow, and blue

2. puffins' beaks   puffins

3. high rocks and cliffs   help puffins swim

4. burrows   where puffins live

5. webbed feet   tunnels dug into grassy slopes

6. chick   eats small fish brought by parents

B. Answer <u>True</u> or <u>False</u>.

1. Puffins are large land birds. _____

2. During the summer, puffins come on land. _____

3. Puffins eat plants. _____

4. Puffins are expert swimmers and divers. _____

5. Puffins have small heads, long necks, and thin bodies. _____

6. Puffins spend most of their time at sea. _____

C. Fill in the missing words.

1. Puffins use their wings and _____ to swim underwater. (webbed feet, triangular beaks)

2. During the mating season, puffins have red, yellow, and blue _____. (breasts, beaks)

3. Puffins can _____ from the air into the ocean. (dive, jump)

4. Puffins can catch _____ small fish in their large beaks in a single dive. (many, one)

5. After the egg hatches, the chick stays in the burrow for about _____. (40 days, 2 years)

6. Puffins lay eggs in burrows dug into grassy slopes near the _____. (forests, shore)

Ducks

Mallard Ducks

Ducks live near salt water or fresh water all over the world. Ducks have webbed feet. This feature helps them swim and dive for food. Most ducks eat water plants, seeds, and grains. Some eat small water animals and insects.

There are many kinds of ducks. The mallard is a common wild duck. It is about the size of a chicken. The males often have shiny blue or green heads and necks. Their feathers can be many colors. The females are mostly brown. Mallards migrate to warmer climates in winter.

The muscovy is a larger duck. It lives in warm places such as Florida. The muscovy is sometimes called the "ugly duck." It is usually black and white. Females and males have the same coloring. Muscovies have knobby red skin on their faces and the backs of their necks. These ducks are very tame. They like bread and most household leftover foods.

Ducks have a layer of feathers called down. Down is very soft and thick. It helps keep ducks warm. Most ducks build their nests on the ground. Some muscovies build nests in trees. Female ducks line their nests with the soft down. Most lay 5 to 12 eggs that hatch in about a month. The ducklings can swim and find food the day after they hatch. The mother stays with them until they can fly. They can fly when they are 5 to 8 weeks old.

A. Answer True or False.

1. Ducks can only be found living in dry desert areas. _____

2. Ducks live near fresh water and salt water. _____

3. Most ducks build their nests on the ground. _____

4. The feathers of male mallard ducks can be many colors. _____

5. The muscovy is about the size of a chicken. _____

6. There is only one kind of duck. _____

7. Female and male muscovy ducks have the same coloring.

_____

B. Use the words below to complete the sentences.

dive	eggs	necks
down	fly	nests
ducklings	male	webbed feet

1. Ducks use their _____ to swim and dive for food.

2. Female ducks line their _____ with soft down.

3. Ducks have a layer of feathers called _____ .

4. Female ducks lay 5 to 12 _____ that hatch in about a month.

5. The _____ mallard may have a shiny blue or green head and neck. Its feathers can be many colors.

6. Muscovies have knobby red skin on their faces and the backs of their _____ .

7. Ducks live near salt water or fresh water. They swim and _____ for food.

8. The _____ can swim and find food the day after they hatch.

9. Ducklings cannot _____ until they are 5 to 8 weeks old.

Herons

Great Blue Heron

Herons are wading birds that are found in shallow water throughout the world. They have long, pointed bills and long, thin necks. Herons have stocky bodies with short tails. Because they wade or stand in water, their legs are long and thin. Herons have large, thin feet that help them to stand in mud.

Herons may have white, brown, gray-blue, or black feathers. They fly slowly with their long legs trailing behind them and their heads curled up between their shoulders. The great blue heron is found throughout the United States. This graceful bird stands 4 feet high and has a 6-foot wing span.

A heron may stand for hours with its head between its shoulders. It looks like it is sleeping but it is really waiting for fish. When a fish swims by, the heron strikes quickly to catch it. Herons also wade through water to catch frogs, snakes, insects, or shellfish.

Herons nest in colonies. Their nests, made of sticks, are built in treetops. The female lays 3 to 6 eggs. Parents feed the young herons until they can fly.

Underline the correct words.

1. Herons have large, thin feet that help them to stand in (mud, sand).

2. Herons strike (slowly, quickly) to catch fish.

Part A

Fill in the missing words.

1. Birds are vertebrates, or animals with _____. (backbones, scales)

2. Birds are the only animals with _____. (lungs, feathers)

3. Not all birds can _____. (breathe, fly)

4. Because gulls eat any garbage or food that floats, they help keep the water _____. (dirty, clean)

5. Penguins cannot fly but are excellent _____. (swimmers, waders)

6. Puffins are sometimes called sea parrots because of their large, triangular _____. (beaks, wings)

7. Female ducks line their nests with _____. (sticks, down)

8. Herons are _____ birds. (wading, diving)

9. Flamingos are large _____ water birds. (green, pink)

Part B

Underline the correct words.

1. Most water birds (swim, walk) to find food.

2. Some water birds live in large groups called (herds, flocks).

3. Many gulls migrate south to warmer areas in the (winter, summer).

4. Kingfishers spear fish with their long, pointed (legs, bills).

5. Flamingos are tall birds that (wade, dive) to find food.

6. Penguins have feathers and (a nest, fat) to help keep them warm.

7. Ducks use their (long bills, webbed feet) to swim or dive for food.

8. Because herons wade or stand in water, their legs are (short, long).

Explore How Feathers Work

You Need

- 2 sheets of paper
- scissors
- petroleum jelly
- container of water

1. Water birds have a coat of special oil on their feathers. This oil makes the feathers waterproof. This is an adaptation that helps the birds to stay dry and warm. Find out how this works.

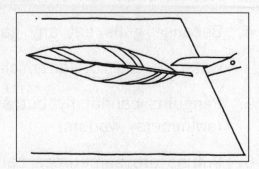

2. Draw a large feather on each sheet of paper as shown. Cut out both feathers.

3. Spread a very thin coat of petroleum jelly on both sides of one feather. Do not coat the other feather.

4. Compare the feathers. How are they alike? How are they different?

5. Quickly dip both feathers into a container of water. Compare the feathers again. Have they changed? How are they alike and different?

Write the Answer

Explain how feathers without oil would change the life of a water bird.

_____

_____

_____

Fill in the circle in front of the word or phrase that best completes each sentence. The first one is done for you.

1. The male mallard duck is more colorful than the
   - ⓐ flamingo.
   - ● female duck.
   - ⓒ other birds.

2. The flamingo and the heron wade to find
   - ⓐ food.
   - ⓑ mates.
   - ⓒ chicks.

3. The nests of flamingos are
   - ⓐ large mud mounds.
   - ⓑ made of sand.
   - ⓒ burrows dug in cliffs.

4. The end of the bill of the kingfisher is pointed for
   - ⓐ carrying fish.
   - ⓑ filtering food.
   - ⓒ spearing fish.

5. Ducks dive to find
   - ⓐ food.
   - ⓑ nests.
   - ⓒ chicks.

6. A penguin has fat under its skin to keep it
   - ⓐ dry.
   - ⓑ soft.
   - ⓒ warm.

Fill in the missing words.

7. Birds are the only animals that have _____.
   (feathers, fur)

8. Puffins live along _____.
   (rivers, northern seacoasts)

9. All birds are _____-blooded. (cold, warm)

Write the answer on the lines.

10. Explain how penguins swim.

_____

_____

UNIT 7
Water Mammals

Porpoise

Walrus

What Is a Mammal?

There are more than 4,000 kinds of mammals. Dogs, cats, horses, and giraffes are land **mammals.** There are also mammals, such as whales, porpoises, and seals, that live in the water.

Every animal has **adaptations** that help it live in its environment. Water mammals have many adaptations, such as their shape or a special part of their body, that help them live in their water environment. Whales are water mammals that have flippers and tails that help them swim through the water. Otters have long toes with claws that help them dig and hold food. Manatees have special mouths and teeth that help them eat plants.

All mammals are alike in some ways. Mammals are vertebrates, or animals with backbones. They are warm-blooded like birds. Most mammals have some hair or fur. Many mammals, like the otter, have a thick coat of fur. But some, like the walrus, have only a few whiskers around their mouths. Mammals also breathe air with lungs.

Most young mammals develop inside their mother's body and are born alive. Mammals are different from all other animals because they have special glands that produce milk to feed their young. Mammals also have more developed brains than other animals. So young mammals are able to learn more than other young animals. They stay with their parents for a long time while the parents protect and teach them.

A. Answer True or False.

1. Mammals are cold-blooded like reptiles. _____

2. Mammals are vertebrates, or animals with backbones. _____

3. Mammals breathe air with lungs. _____

4. Every animal has adaptations that help it live in its environment. _____

5. Water mammals do not have any adaptations. _____

6. Most young mammals hatch from eggs. _____

7. Mammals have glands that produce milk to feed their young. _____

8. Young mammals are able to learn more than other animals. _____

9. Mammals take care of themselves as soon as they are born. _____

10. Most mammals have hair or fur. _____

B. Draw lines to match each mammal with its description.

1. walruses   flippers and tails to help them swim

2. whales   a few whiskers around their mouths

3. otters   special mouths and teeth

4. manatees   long toes with claws that help them dig

C. Use each word to write a sentence about mammals.

1. warm-blooded _____

_____

2. adaptations _____

_____

109

Whales

Killer Whale

Most whales live in salt water, but some small whales live in fresh water. The water around whales is colder than their body temperature. So whales have special adaptations to keep them warm. Thick layers of fat called **blubber** help whales stay warm. Whales that live in icy waters can have blubber that is 20 inches thick. Warm-water whales have only 6 inches of blubber.

The shape of their thick bodies is another adaptation that helps whales keep warm. Their thick bodies trap heat. Whales also have thick flippers and fins that do not lose much heat as they swim.

When they are on the surface, whales breathe air through **blowholes** on the tops of their heads. Before they dive, whales fill their lungs with air and close their blowholes. Many whales can stay underwater for an hour. When whales surface, they blow the old air out of their blowholes in a watery spray.

Whales are divided into two groups, **baleen whales** and **toothed whales.** Baleen whales have bony plates, or baleen, in their mouths. The baleen filters food from the sea. Blue whales are baleen whales. They can grow to be 100 feet long. But these huge mammals feed only on tiny plankton.

Most whales are toothed whales. Some toothed whales have very few teeth. But killer whales have 48 pointed teeth that they use to catch food, not chew it. Killer whales travel in groups called **pods** to find their food. They eat large fish, squid, small seals, dolphins, and walruses.

A. Use the words below to complete the sentences.

| baleen | blubber | plankton |
| blowholes | fins | toothed |

1. Thick layers of fat called _____ help keep whales warm.

2. Some whales have bony plates, or _____, in their mouths.

3. Baleen whales feed only on tiny _____.

4. Most whales are _____ whales.

5. Whales have thick flippers and _____ that do not lose much heat.

6. Whales breathe through _____ on the tops of their heads.

B. Answer True or False.

1. All whales live in fresh water. _____

2. Whales breathe air through blowholes. _____

3. Many whales can stay underwater for an hour. _____

4. Killer whales travel in groups to find their food. _____

C. Write the letter for the correct answer.

1. Whales are _____.
   (a) fish   (b) mammals   (c) reptiles

2. Most whales live in _____.
   (a) fresh water   (b) lakes   (c) salt water

3. Whales come to the surface to _____.
   (a) drink   (b) breathe   (c) die

4. Killer whales have many _____.
   (a) teeth   (b) fins   (c) blowholes

5. Whales that live in icy waters have blubber that is _____.
   (a) 20 inches thick   (b) 2 inches thick   (c) 20 feet thick

Kinds of Whales

Humpback Whale

Blue whales are the largest animals that have ever lived. A blue whale can weigh as much as 1,600 people. Most blue whales grow to be about 85 feet long. Blue whales eat only plankton and are not dangerous to people.

Not all whales are huge. Many of the toothed whales, such as white whales and river dolphins, are about 10 feet long. White whales are milky white and have a bulge on the top of their heads called a **melon.** Many whales have a poor sense of sight and smell. But they have a good sense of hearing. Whales make sounds and then listen for the echoes. In this way, they can find food and one another. In whales, porpoises, and dolphins, the melon helps send and locate the echoes.

The sounds that humpback whales make are called whale songs. Each humpback has a special order for its sounds. It sings them in the same order each time. As a whale gets older, its song becomes longer. The sounds may help whales find mates.

Sperm whales are the largest toothed whales. They grow up to 60 feet long. Sperm whales have huge, square-shaped heads. Male sperm whales have been known to use their powerful heads to ram and sink whaling ships. Sperm whales have teeth only on their lower jaw. They can dive to great depths to find food. Sperm whales feed on squid and sharks.

A. Write the letter for the correct answer.

1. _____ are the largest animals that have ever lived.
   (a) White whales   (b) Blue whales   (c) Killer whales

2. Blue whales eat _____ .
   (a) plankton   (b) people   (c) seals

3. White whales have a bulge on top of their heads called _____ .
   (a) fins   (b) flippers   (c) a melon

4. Humpback whales make sounds called whale _____ .
   (a) noise   (b) songs   (c) echoes

5. Sperm whales have huge, _____ heads.
   (a) square-shaped   (b) pointed   (c) round

6. Whales have a good sense of _____ .
   (a) sight   (b) smell   (c) hearing

B. Draw lines to match each term with its description.

1. blue whales   10 feet long

2. river dolphins   make sounds called whale songs

3. humpback whales   weigh as much as 1,600 people

4. white whales   largest toothed whales

5. sperm whales   have a bulge called a melon on their heads

C. Answer True or False.

1. All whales are huge. _____

2. Blue whales are dangerous to people. _____

3. Whales make sounds and then listen for the echoes. _____

4. As humpback whales get older, their songs get shorter. _____

5. Sperm whales have teeth only on their lower jaw. _____

6. Most blue whales grow to be about 85 feet long. _____

7. All whales eat plankton. _____

Dolphins and Porpoises

Bottle-Nosed Dolphin

Common Porpoise

Dolphins and porpoises are toothed whales. They have streamlined bodies and powerful tails that help them to move easily through the water. Like other whales, dolphins and porpoises have a layer of blubber that keeps them warm.

Dolphins and porpoises are alike in many ways. The main differences in these two mammals is the shape of their snouts and teeth. Dolphins have beaklike snouts and cone-shaped teeth. Porpoises have rounded snouts and flat teeth.

Common dolphins grow to be about 7 feet long. They have black backs, gray sides, and white bellies. Common dolphins live in warm waters and often follow ships for miles.

Bottle-nosed dolphins are the most familiar dolphins. They may grow to be 12 feet long. Bottle-nosed dolphins are gray. These dolphins are very social and seem to be very friendly toward people.

Killer whales are the largest kind of dolphin. They can grow to be 30 feet long. Killer whales travel in pods and are often found in colder northern waters.

Porpoises are smaller than dolphins. The largest porpoises are 6 feet long. Common porpoises have black backs and white bellies. Unlike dolphins, porpoises avoid people and often travel alone.

Dolphins and porpoises are intelligent animals. They communicate with each other by making chirping sounds. Many dolphins and porpoises live in groups that play and hunt for food together. They help members in the group that are in trouble.

A. Use the words below to complete the sentences.

blubber	people	teeth
largest	snouts	toothed

1. Dolphins and porpoises are _____ whales.

2. Dolphins and porpoises have a layer of _____ that keeps them warm.

3. Dolphins have beaklike _____ and cone-shaped teeth.

4. Porpoises have rounded snouts and flat _____.

5. Killer whales are the _____ kind of dolphin.

6. Unlike dolphins, porpoises avoid _____ and travel alone.

B. Answer True or False.

1. Bottle-nosed dolphins seem to be friendly toward people. _____

2. Dolphins and porpoises are alike in many ways. _____

3. Dolphins are much smaller than porpoises. _____

4. Dolphins and porpoises are intelligent animals. _____

5. Dolphins and porpoises help members in their group that are in trouble. _____

C. Underline the correct words.

1. The bottle-nosed dolphin is (many colors, gray).

2. Dolphins may follow (ships, birds).

3. Many dolphins and porpoises live in groups that play and hunt for (people, food) together.

4. Dolphins and porpoises (fight, communicate) with each other by making chirping sounds.

5. Killer whales travel in pods and are often found in (warmer, colder) northern waters.

Seals

Harbor Seal

Fur Seals

Seals are excellent swimmers and divers. Some can swim 15 miles an hour and others can dive 2,000 feet underwater. Most seals live in polar regions.

Seals have adaptations that help them live in cold water. Most have sleek, fur-covered bodies. Under their fur, they have a layer of blubber that helps them stay warm. Also, most seals spread oil over their fur to make it waterproof. Seals have short legs that end in flippers.

There are two groups of seals, earless seals and eared seals. Earless seals do not have any ears showing on the outside of their heads. Earless seals include elephant seals and harbor seals. The largest seals, elephant seals, can be 20 feet long and weigh up to 8,000 pounds. They are clumsy on land, but fast and graceful in the water. Harbor seals are about 6 feet long and weigh about 250 pounds. They can be found in northern oceans. Some live in rivers and lakes.

Eared seals have tiny ears on the outside of their heads. These seals include sea lions and northern fur seals. Some sea lions live in the Pacific Ocean, along the coast of North America. They dive for fish and squid. They come to shore and live in colonies to have their young.

Northern fur seals breed only on a few islands near Alaska. They go back to the same island every summer. During the winter, the seals live in the ocean, thousands of miles from the islands.

A. Answer True or False.

1. Seals are poor swimmers and divers. _____

2. Most seals live in polar regions. _____

3. Most seals have fur-covered bodies. _____

4. All seals have ears on the outside of their heads. _____

5. Blubber helps seals stay warm. _____

B. Write elephant seal, northern fur seal, or both after each phrase.

1. breeds on islands near Alaska _____

2. has flippers _____

3. can weigh up to 8,000 pounds _____

4. has ears on outside of its head _____

5. has a layer of blubber _____

C. Write the letter for the correct answer.

1. A layer of _____ helps seals stay warm.
   (a) skin   (b) scales   (c) blubber

2. Seals spread oil over their fur to make it _____.
   (a) waterproof   (b) flat   (c) sticky

3. Some seals can swim _____ miles an hour.
   (a) 200   (b) 50   (c) 15

4. One kind of earless seal is the _____.
   (a) northern fur seal   (b) harbor seal   (c) sea lion

D. Use each word to write a sentence about seals.

1. earless _____

_____

2. colonies _____

_____

Walruses

Walruses

A Herd of Walruses

Walruses are water mammals that live in the icy waters of the Arctic Ocean. An adult male walrus may be 12 feet long and weigh up to 3,000 pounds. Walruses are protected from the cold by a thick layer of blubber and by a thick, wrinkled, almost hairless skin. However, walruses have thick whiskers on their upper lip that are sensitive to touch. They use their whiskers to help them find food.

Walruses have powerful flippers that help them to be excellent swimmers. They spend much of their time swimming along the ocean bottom looking for clams, their favorite food.

Both male and female walruses have long, white **tusks** that grow from their upper jaws. Walruses use their tusks to pull themselves up out of the water and onto the ice. When they are underwater, they use their tusks to break a hole in the ice so they can breathe. Walruses also use their tusks to defend themselves against enemies, such as polar bears and killer whales.

The tusks of adult walruses are usually about 10 to 15 inches long. But some walruses have tusks that are 40 inches long. Most walruses live in large groups called **herds.** The male with the largest tusks is usually the leader of the herd.

Walruses are very social animals. Large herds of walruses gather on rocky shores or pieces of floating ice. Female walruses give birth to a single **calf,** or baby walrus. The females then feed and care for their young for about 2 years.

A. Answer <u>True</u> or <u>False</u>.

1. Walruses are land mammals. _____

2. Walruses live in warm water. _____

3. Walruses use their tusks to pull themselves out of the water.

   _____

4. Walruses are excellent swimmers. _____

B. Write the letter for the correct answer.

1. The tusks of adult walruses are usually about _____ long.
   (a) 80 to 100 inches   (b) 7 to 8 feet   (c) 10 to 15 inches

2. The male with the largest _____ is usually the leader of the herd.
   (a) flippers   (b) tusks   (c) whiskers

3. Walruses use their whiskers to help them find _____ .
   (a) ice   (b) water   (c) food

4. Female walruses feed and care for their young for about _____ .
   (a) 4 days   (b) 2 years   (c) 6 weeks

C. Use the words below to complete the sentences.

calf	hairless	tusks
clams	herds	whiskers

1. Walruses have thick, wrinkled, almost _____ skin.

2. Walruses swim along the ocean bottom looking for _____ .

3. Most walruses live in large groups called _____ .

4. Walruses have thick _____ on their upper lips.

5. Female walruses give birth to a single _____ , or baby walrus.

6. Both male and female walruses have _____ .

Sea Otters and River Otters

Sea Otter

River Otter

Otters are small mammals that live mostly in water. Their long, slender bodies are made for swimming. They have small, streamlined heads with small, round ears and short snouts. Their ears and noses close tightly when they are underwater. An otter's back legs are long and shaped like a paddle. Its tail is thick and flat on the underside and helps to steer the otter as it swims. Many otters also have webbed toes that are good for paddling in water.

Otters have bodies that are covered with fur to help them stay warm in water. The hairs are so tightly packed together that the fur is waterproof.

Otters have very sensitive toes and paws that help them to hold their food. Because they are so active, otters must eat many times a day. Otters eat frogs, shellfish, and fish.

Sea otters live in salt water. They can grow to be 4 feet long and weigh about 80 pounds. They have dark brown fur. They are one of the few animals that use tools. A sea otter can float on its back and hold a rock on its chest. Then, it hammers a shellfish against the rock to break open the shell.

River otters live on land and in fresh water. Most river otters are about the same length as sea otters but they weigh less. They have dark brown fur. River otters move from stream to stream looking for fish and crayfish to eat. River otters are found in most places in the world, except Australia and Antarctica.

A. Answer True or False.

1. Sea otters live in fresh water. _____

2. Otters have bodies that are covered with fur. _____

3. River otters live in the ocean. _____

4. River otters eat fish and shellfish. _____

5. Sea otters are fish. _____

6. River otters move from stream to stream looking for fish. _____

7. Sea otters are one of the few animals that cannot use tools. _____

8. River otters are found in Antarctica. _____

B. Choose the phrases that describe otters. Write them on the lines.

big ears	slender bodies	use tools
fins	small heads	waterproof fur
long snouts	thick, flat tail	webbed toes

1. _____

2. _____

3. _____

4. _____

5. _____

6. _____

C. Answer the question.

How does a sea otter use tools? _____

_____

_____

_____

The Manatee

A Manatee

The manatee, or sea cow, is a water mammal that is found in quiet harbors, bays, and rivers. Manatees live in the warm, shallow waters near Florida and Central and South America.

Manatees usually have gray bodies with little or no hair. Their heavy bodies have only two legs and a flat, rounded tail. Like walruses, manatees have thick, wrinkled skin. They are about 15 feet long and can weigh 1,500 pounds.

Manatees have been called gentle giants because they are harmless. They eat only plants. They are usually very shy and swim away from danger.

Manatees have poor eyesight, but they hear very well. Female manatees can hear calves, or young, when they are 200 feet away. Their calves make squeaks or squeals when they are afraid.

A female manatee may have a calf every 5 years. The calf is born in water, but may rest on its mother's back and stay above water for a short time. Calves spend their first 2 years drinking mother's milk and nibbling grass with adult females.

Manatees are important to people because they eat water plants that clog canals and lakes. They rip and tear plants off the bottom with their upper lips. They take in mouthfuls of water plants and sand at the same time. In this way, the manatee's teeth get worn down. The old teeth move forward and then fall out. They are replaced by new teeth. Manatees eat up to 100 pounds of food a day.

A. **Draw lines to match each term with its description.**

1. teeth   where some manatees live

2. Florida   get worn down

3. upper lips   another name for the manatee

4. sea cow   rip and tear plants off the bottom

5. calf   flat and rounded

6. tail   young manatee

B. **Answer True or False.**

1. Manatees have thick, wrinkled skin. _____

2. Manatees are dangerous to people. _____

3. Manatee calves are born on land. _____

4. Manatees eat water plants that clog canals. _____

5. Teeth are always being replaced in a manatee's mouth. _____

6. Manatees have very good eyesight. _____

C. **Write the letter for the correct answer.**

1. Manatees live in _____ waters.
   (a) warm, shallow   (b) Arctic   (c) cold, deep

2. Manatees have gray bodies with _____.
   (a) long feathers   (b) thick fur   (c) little hair

3. Manatees eat only _____.
   (a) plants   (b) fish   (c) shrimp

4. Calves make squeaks when they are _____.
   (a) born   (b) bored   (c) afraid

5. A female manatee may have a calf every _____.
   (a) 5 years   (b) year   (c) 6 months

6. Calves spend their first 2 years drinking milk and _____.
   (a) fishing   (b) nibbling grass   (c) fighting

The Platypus

A Platypus

The platypus is one of the few mammals that lays eggs. It lives in burrows along rivers and streams in Australia. The platypus hunts in water for the worms and shellfish it eats.

The platypus has many adaptations that help it live in its environment. Its snout is 2 to 6 inches long with nostrils on the top. The platypus uses its nostrils to smell food under water. Then it uses its snout to scoop up the food. Because its snout looks like the bill of a duck, the platypus is sometimes called the duckbill.

The platypus is covered with thick, brown fur that helps it stay warm when it swims. It has four short legs with webbed feet that are good for swimming. But when it needs to dig a burrow, the platypus can pull back the webbing between its toes and use its long claws to dig.

Platypuses live in burrows. But when a female platypus is about to lay eggs, she digs a longer burrow. Then she lays two or three eggs. After they hatch, young platypuses are carefully watched and fed milk by their mothers.

Underline the correct words.

1. The platypus is one of the few (mammals, birds) that lays eggs.

2. The platypus has a snout shaped like a (duck's bill, bottle).

Part A

Use the words below to complete the sentences.

baleen	environment	tools
blubber	flippers	toothed
blue whale	manatee	tusks

1. Every animal has adaptations that help it live in its _____.

2. Some whales have _____, or bony plates, in their mouths.

3. Dolphins and porpoises are _____ whales.

4. A layer of fat, or _____, helps many water mammals stay warm.

5. The _____ is the largest animal that has ever lived.

6. Both male and female walruses have _____.

7. The sea cow, or _____, eats only plants.

8. The otter is one of the few animals that can use _____.

9. Seals have short legs that end in _____.

Part B

Underline the correct words.

1. Mammals are (warm-blooded, cold-blooded) vertebrates.

2. Whales take in air through a (fin, blowhole) on the top of their heads.

3. Most whales live in (salt water, fresh water).

4. Most seals live in (warm regions, polar regions).

5. Otters have long (arms, bodies) made for swimming.

6. Platypuses are one of the few mammals that (use tools, lay eggs).

Facts on Water Mammals

You Need

- a partner
- paper
- encyclopedia or books on water mammals
- a tape measure

1. Look through pages 108–124. Choose one of the water mammals to write about.

2. Make a chart like the one shown here. Leave room above the chart for a picture of your water mammal.

3. Give the information called for on your chart about your water mammal. Use books on water mammals or use an encyclopedia to find information about your mammal that you cannot find in your book.

4. Draw or trace a picture of your water mammal in the space above the chart.

5. Work with your partner and measure each other's arm span from fingertip to fingertip. Record this number. Is your arm span longer than the water mammal you chose to study?

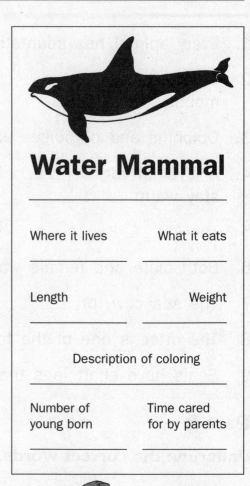

Water Mammal

Where it lives   What it eats

Length   Weight

Description of coloring

Number of   Time cared
young born   for by parents

Write the Answer

How many of you would have to stand with arms open wide, fingertip to fingertip, to equal the length of your water mammal? Explain your answer.

Fill in the circle in front of the word or phrase that best completes each sentence. The first one is done for you.

1. Walruses live in
   - (a) rivers and lakes.
   - (b) warm oceans.
   - ● the icy Arctic Ocean.

2. The platypus is one of the few mammals that
   - (a) swims.
   - (b) lays eggs.
   - (c) lives in water.

3. Every animal has adaptations that help it live in
   - (a) a nest.
   - (b) its environment.
   - (c) the ocean.

4. The bony plates in a whale's mouth are called
   - (a) plankton.
   - (b) baleen.
   - (c) blowhole.

5. Dolphins and porpoises are
   - (a) seals.
   - (b) baleen whales.
   - (c) toothed whales.

6. Most seals have bodies covered with
   - (a) fur.
   - (b) feathers.
   - (c) leather.

Fill in the missing words.

7. River otters eat _____. (plants, fish)

8. The manatee eats only _____. (dolphins, plants)

9. Mammals are warm-blooded _____. (vertebrates, invertebrates)

Write the answer on the lines.

10. How do whales stay warm in icy water?

_____

_____

UNIT 8
Conservation

Water in the Environment

An environment has many parts.

The environment of a plant or an animal is made up of everything around it. Other plants and animals, air, water, land, sunlight, and temperature can all be part of an environment.

An environment affects the plants and animals living in it. It also affects other environments. If harmful chemicals are released into the air, the wind can blow them into other environments miles away.

Water is an especially important part of Earth's environments. All living things need water. But there is only a certain amount of water on Earth. We use this water over and over again.

Water moves from one environment to another. If there are harmful chemicals in the air, rain picks them up as it falls. The rain soaks into the ground, carrying the chemicals with it. If people drink this underground water, they also drink the harmful chemicals. If crops are grown in this ground, the chemicals end up in the plants.

Sometimes rain that has picked up harmful chemicals in the air falls in lakes and rivers. The chemicals then spread out in the lakes and rivers. They can harm the fish that live there. The rivers can also carry them out into the ocean.

A. **Use the words below to complete the sentences.**

animals	Earth's	living
certain	environment	

1. The _____ of a plant or animal is made up of everything around it.

2. An environment affects the plants and _____ living in it.

3. All _____ things need water.

4. Water is an especially important part of _____ environments.

5. There is only a _____ amount of water on Earth.

B. **List six things that can be part of an environment.**

1. _____

2. _____

3. _____

4. _____

5. _____

6. _____

C. **Answer True or False.**

1. Water moves from one environment to another. _____

2. If harmful chemicals are released into the air, the wind can blow them miles away. _____

3. Plants and animals are not part of an environment. _____

4. There is only a certain amount of water on Earth. _____

5. Rain cannot pick up harmful chemicals from the air. _____

Water Pollution

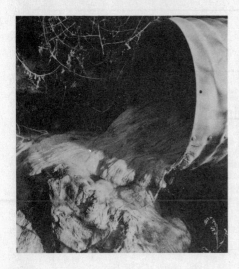

Oil spills and litter are two causes of water pollution.

Polluting the environment means making it dirty. People are polluting every part of the environment. This pollution is unhealthy for people and other living things.

Water is one part of the environment that is being polluted. Because of pollution, there is less water on Earth that is safe for drinking and swimming. Water pollution can kill animals that live in the water. It can also make them unsafe to eat. Because all environments affect each other, water pollution harms all living things.

In the United States, industry is the greatest polluter of water. Thousands of factories dump waste materials into rivers and oceans. These waste materials often contain poisons and other harmful chemicals. Some cities allow sewage to be dumped into the water before the sewage has been treated to make it safe. Oil companies have spilled oil into the oceans by accident. The oil kills water plants and animals. Waste material from nuclear power plants can also leak into water by accident. Nuclear waste material can cause cancer in people.

Remember that there is only a certain amount of water on Earth. We need to stop polluting our water, and clean up water that is polluted. Then we will have clean water to use in the future.

A. Fill in the missing words.

1. Polluting the environment means making it _____. (clean, dirty)

2. Pollution is _____ for people and other living things. (healthy, unhealthy)

3. In the United States, _____ the greatest polluter of water. (industry is, trees are)

4. Because of water pollution, there is _____ water on Earth that is safe for drinking and swimming. (less, more)

5. Pollution can _____ animals that live in the water. (kill, help)

B. Draw lines to match the kind of pollution with its source.

1. oil companies   dump poisons and chemicals

2. factories   oil spills that kill water life

3. cities   wastes that can cause cancer

4. nuclear power plants   dump untreated sewage

C. Answer the questions.

1. Why does water pollution harm all living things? _____

_____

_____

2. Why is it dangerous for waste material from nuclear power plants to leak into the water? _____

_____

D. Answer True or False.

1. Oil companies have spilled oil into the oceans by accident.

_____

2. Pollution is healthy for people and other living things. _____

3. Factories never dump waste materials into rivers and oceans.

_____

131

Animals in Danger

Some countries still hunt whales for food and other products.

Millions of years ago, there were no people on Earth. Earth's environments were very different. Many animals lived on Earth. As time passed, Earth's environments changed. The animals that could not adjust to the new environments became **extinct.** An animal is extinct when every one of its kind has died.

Animals have become extinct in later times, too. People have hunted some kinds of animals until there were none left. The Steller's sea cow was a 9,000-pound sea mammal that was discovered in 1741. Sailors killed the animals for food, and by 1768, they were extinct. Other animals have become extinct because people polluted their environments. Even today, there are animals that are in danger of becoming extinct. These animals are called **endangered animals.**

In Unit 5, you read about green turtles. Green turtles are one of just six kinds of sea turtles. All but one kind are endangered, but people are trying to protect them.

You also read about crocodiles. Thousands of American crocodiles once lived in southern Florida. But many crocodiles were killed for their skins. In 1975, fewer than 20 crocodile nests were counted. Now there are laws against killing crocodiles. By 2003, between 500 and 1,200 crocodiles lived in Florida.

Whales have been hunted and almost made extinct. In 2003, fewer than 2,000 blue whales were alive. Some other endangered water animals are brown pelicans, manatees, and several kinds of seals.

A. Underline the correct words.

1. An animal is (endangered, extinct) when every one of its kind has died.

2. Some animals have become extinct because (nature, people) polluted their environments.

3. Sailors (chased away, killed) the Steller's sea cow for food, and by 1768, they were extinct.

4. Steps have been taken to (protect, kill off) green turtles.

5. Animals that are in danger of becoming extinct are called (water life, endangered animals).

B. List five water animals that are endangered.

1. _____

2. _____

3. _____

4. _____

5. _____

C. Answer True or False.

1. Many crocodiles were killed for their skins. _____

2. People have hunted some kinds of animals until there were none left. _____

3. Today, there are no animals that are in danger of becoming extinct. _____

D. Use each word to write a sentence about animals in danger.

1. extinct _____

_____

2. environment _____

_____

133

Protecting Animals

National wildlife refuges protect water animals.

You have read about laws that protect endangered animals in the United States. These are **conservation** laws. Conservation is the protecting and saving of something. The Ocean Mammal Protection Bill is a conservation law that was passed in 1972. It protects seals, walruses, and other water mammals from being hunted.

But conservation laws are not the only way that water animals and other living things can be protected. Today, the United States has hundreds of **national wildlife refuges.** These refuges are places where animals and their environments are protected. The first wildlife refuge was set up in 1903 on Pelican Island, off the coast of Florida. It protects the brown pelicans that live there.

The **Fish and Wildlife Service** also helps protect water animals. One of its jobs is to take care of fish **hatcheries.** Fish hatcheries are places where fish eggs are hatched.

Answer True or False.

1. Conservation laws are the only way that water animals can be protected. _____

2. National wildlife refuges are places where animals and their environments are protected. _____

134

Part A

Write the letter for the correct answer.

1. Everything around a plant or an animal is part of its _____.
   (a) pollution   (b) environment   (c) conservation

2. Every environment _____ other environments.
   (a) affects   (b) is separate from   (c) harms

3. There is only a certain amount of _____ on Earth.
   (a) plants   (b) animals   (c) water

4. Polluting the environment means making it _____.
   (a) clean   (b) dirty   (c) healthy

5. Because of water pollution, there is _____ water on Earth that is safe.
   (a) no   (b) less   (c) more

6. An animal is extinct when every one of its kind _____.
   (a) has died   (b) is living   (c) is in danger

7. Blue whales and brown pelicans are _____ animals.
   (a) extinct   (b) land   (c) endangered

8. _____ are places where animals and their environments are protected.
   (a) Cities   (b) Wildlife refuges   (c) Factories

Part B

Read each sentence. Write <u>True</u> if the sentence is true. Write <u>False</u> if the sentence is false.

1. The blue whale is almost extinct. _____

2. Oil spilled into oceans kills plants and animals. _____

3. Something that happens in one environment does not affect other environments. _____

4. Nuclear waste material can cause cancer in people. _____

5. Conservation is the protecting and saving of something. _____

6. There are no conservation laws in the United States. _____

Make Your Own Water Filter

You Need

- 2 partners
- water
- 2 small clear plastic cups
- dirt
- sand
- gravel
- small stones
- 2 containers with drainage holes
- tray
- spoon

1. Make a water filter to see how water gets filtered at a water treatment plant.

2. One partner mixes the water and dirt to make dirty water. The other two partners use containers to make a filter.

3. Fill each container with a layer of sand, then a layer of gravel, and then a layer of small stones as shown in the diagram.

4. Place the empty cup on the tray. Two partners hold the containers, one over the other, as shown. Make sure the hole in the bottom container is over the cup.

5. The other partner slowly pours the muddy water into the top container. The water will drain through the two filters and into the cup. Make sure the water drains into the cup. Is it clean?

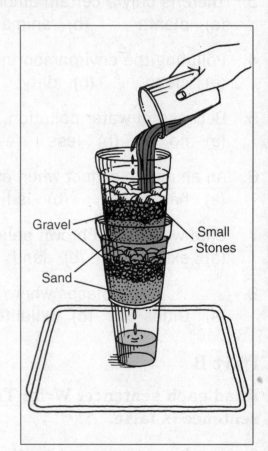

Gravel

Small Stones

Sand

Write the Answer

What would happen if you filtered the water again? Try it.

_____

_____

_____

Fill in the circle in front of the word or phrase that best completes each sentence. The first one is done for you.

1. Water life can be killed by
   ⓐ conservation.
   ● water pollution.
   ⓒ plankton.

2. Air, water, and land can all be part of
   ⓐ an environment.
   ⓑ pollution.
   ⓒ industry.

3. Endangered animals are protected by
   ⓐ water.
   ⓑ conservation laws.
   ⓒ hunting.

4. We use the water on Earth
   ⓐ only once.
   ⓑ just for industry.
   ⓒ over and over again.

5. Some animals that are not endangered are
   ⓐ crocodiles and whales.
   ⓑ seals and walruses.
   ⓒ cats and dogs.

6. Waste material is dumped into rivers and oceans by some
   ⓐ animals.
   ⓑ factories.
   ⓒ wildlife refuges.

Fill in the missing words.

7. Pollution is _____ . (unhealthy, healthy)

8. The environment is being polluted by _____ . (people, water)

9. For centuries whales have been _____ . (protected, hunted)

Write the answer on the lines.

10. Why are wildlife refuges important to animals?

_____

_____

_____

adaptation, page 108.
An adaptation is a shape or a special body part that helps an animal live in its environment. Whales, for example, have flippers and tails that help them swim through the water.

algae, page 18.
Algae make up the largest group of underwater organisms that make their own food. Algae have no roots, stems, leaves, or flowers and are not plants. But they have chlorophyll like plants.

bald cypress, page 26.
The bald cypress is a tree that grows in wet areas from Texas to New Jersey. The crown may be 100 feet across, and the tree may reach a height of 170 feet.

baleen whale, page 110.
A baleen whale has bony plates, or baleen, in its mouth. The baleen filters food from the sea. Blue whales are baleen whales.

bill, page 94.
A bill is the beak, or mouth, of a bird. Bills help birds get their food.

bird, page 90.
A bird is a warm-blooded vertebrate. Birds have wings and are the only animals that have feathers.

blowhole, page 110.
A blowhole is a hole on the top of a whale's head. Whales breathe air through their blowholes.

blubber, page 110.
Blubber is the layer of fat under the skin of some water mammals. Blubber helps water mammals stay warm.

burrow, page 94.
A burrow is a tunnel in the ground made by an animal. Kingfishers dig burrows to prepare a nesting place for their eggs.

calf, page 118.
A calf is the young of certain mammals, such as walruses. Female walruses feed and take care of their calves for about 2 years.

carnivore, page 58.
A carnivore is an animal that eats only meat. Bass are fish that are carnivores.

cartilage, page 52.
Cartilage is a substance that is softer than bone. It makes up the skeletons of sharks and rays.

cells, page 4.
All plants and animals are made of small parts called cells. Cells are mostly water.

chlorophyll, page 18.
Chlorophyll is the green matter that helps plants to make their own food.

coelenterate, page 43.
A coelenterate is a kind of invertebrate water animal. Some of the world's most colorful and beautiful sea animals, such as sea anemones, coral animals, and jellyfish, are coelenterates.

cold-blooded, page 52.
Cold-blooded means that the body temperature of an animal changes with the temperature of the air or water around it. Most fish are cold-blooded.

colony, page 44.
A colony is a group of animals that live together. Coral animals live in very large colonies.

conservation, page 134.
Conservation is the protecting and saving of something. Conservation laws protect endangered animals, such as seals and walruses, from being hunted.

coral reef, page 44.
A coral reef is a wall formed when large colonies of coral animals grow together. Coral reefs are found only in warm salt water.

crest, page 94.
A crest is a group of feathers that stick up on the head of a bird. Kingfishers are birds that have crests.

crustacean, page 40.
A crustacean is an invertebrate water animal with a shell. Crustaceans have bodies made of separate parts that are joined together and several pairs of jointed legs. Lobsters and crabs are crustaceans.

current, page 10.

A current is like a river moving through ocean waters. Some currents are warmer than the water around them. Others are colder. Currents affect the temperature of nearby land.

D

deep current, page 10.

A deep current is an ocean current caused by differences in water temperature. Deep currents sometimes come to the ocean's surface bringing up minerals from the ocean floor.

down, page 92.

Down is a layer of soft, thick feathers. Young gulls are covered with down. Ducks have a layer of down under their outer feathers.

duckweed, page 20.

Duckweed is a perennial water plant that has no true leaves or stems. It provides food for many ducks and other water birds. One kind of duckweed is the smallest flowering plant known.

E

endangered animal, page 132.

An endangered animal is one that is in danger of becoming extinct, or dying out. The blue whale, brown pelican, and sea otter are endangered animals.

environment, page 4.

An environment is a place where plants and animals live.

extinct, page 132.

An animal is extinct when every one of its kind has died. The Steller's sea cow is an extinct water mammal.

F

fangs, page 79.

Fangs are the long, sharp teeth of poisonous snakes. When a poisonous snake bites, venom goes through its fangs.

feathers, page 90.

Feathers are the covering of a bird's body. They keep a bird warm and help it to fly. Birds are the only animals with feathers.

fin, page 52.

A fin is a part of a fish that is found along the back, stomach, and sides. Fish use their fins to swim and to keep balanced.

Fish and Wildlife Service, page 134.

The Fish and Wildlife Service is a United States government agency that helps protect animals. One job of the Fish and Wildlife Service is taking care of fish hatcheries.

flock, page 90.

A flock is a large group of birds. Many water birds live in flocks.

food chain, page 12.

A food chain describes the way that different living things depend on each other for food. There are food chains in both land and water environments. All food chains start with plants.

foot, page 34.

A foot is a muscle under the body of a clam. The foot helps the clam to move. It also acts as an anchor to keep the clam in one place.

fresh water, page 6.

Water in streams, rivers, lakes, and ponds is fresh water. Fresh water does not have as much dissolved salt as ocean water.

frond, page 20.

A frond is a leaflike part of a plant. Duckweed is a plant that has fronds that float on the surface of ponds.

G

gills, page 32.

Gills are body parts that let fish and other water animals take in oxygen that is dissolved in water.

H

hatchery, page 134.

A hatchery is a place where fish eggs are hatched.

herd, page 118.

A herd is a large group of animals. Most walruses live in herds.

I

invertebrate, page 30.

An invertebrate is an animal that does not have a backbone. Many different kinds of invertebrate animals, such as mollusks, crustaceans, and coelenterates, live in water.

K

kelp, page 18.

Kelp is a kind of large brown algae that can grow to be 200 feet long. It has ribbonlike blades that float in the ocean.

knee, page 26.

A knee is a growth on the roots of a bald cypress tree. Knees can grow to be about 6 feet tall.

L **ligament,** page 34.

A ligament is a hard tissue that acts like a hinge to open and close the parts of a clam's shell.

M **mammal,** page 108.

A mammal is a warm-blooded vertebrate. Most mammals have some hair or fur. They breathe air with lungs. The young of most mammals are born alive. They feed on milk from their mother's body. Some mammals, such as whales and seals, live in the water.

mangrove, page 24.

A mangrove is a tree that grows in salt water in warm, wet places. Red mangroves grow from the coast of Florida all the way to South America.

melon, page 112.

A melon is a bulge on the top of a white whale's head. The melon helps send and locate sounds that whales make.

migrate, page 64.

To migrate means to travel to different environments in different seasons. Tuna migrate in schools to colder water in summer. They come back to warmer water in the fall.

mollusk, page 32.

A mollusk is an invertebrate water animal with a soft body. Some mollusks, like snails, have one-part shells. Others, like clams, have two-part shells. Some, like the octopus, have no shells at all.

molt, page 40.

To molt means to shed, or get rid of, a shell and to grow a new one. As crabs and lobsters grow, they molt.

N **national wildlife refuge,** page 134.

A national wildlife refuge is a place where animals and their environments are protected. The United States has hundreds of wildlife refuges, such as Pelican Island in Florida.

nest, page 90.

A nest is a place where a bird lays its eggs. It may be made of twigs or mud. It may also be a hole in a tree or in the dirt.

nonpoisonous, page 78.

A nonpoisonous animal is one whose bite or sting does not have a poison. Some freshwater snakes are nonpoisonous.

O **omnivore,** page 84.

An omnivore is an animal that eats plants as well as other animals. Snapping turtles are omnivores.

organisms, page 21.

Organisms are living things.

P **perennial,** page 20.

A perennial plant is one that lives year after year. Duckweed is a perennial.

plankton, page 8.

Plankton are tiny living things at the surface of the ocean. They are food for many saltwater animals, even huge whales.

pod, page 110.

A pod is a group of killer whales. Killer whales travel in pods to find their food.

poisonous, page 76.

A poisonous animal is one whose bite or sting has a poison that can kill or injure other animals. All sea snakes are poisonous.

polluting, page 130.

Polluting means making the environment dirty. Pollution is unhealthy for people and other living things.

R **reptile,** page 74.

A reptile is a cold-blooded vertebrate. All reptiles have lungs. Their bodies are covered with dry scales or hard plates. Most reproduce by laying eggs on land. Water reptiles, such as alligators and turtles, spend at least part of their lives in water.

rookery, page 98.

A rookery is a place where colonies, or groups of birds, raise their young. There may be as many as one million penguins in a rookery.

S **salt water,** page 6.

The water in oceans is salt water. Salt water has large amounts of dissolved salts.

scales, page 52.

Scales are thin plates that cover the body of a fish. The bodies of some reptiles are covered with hard scales.

school, page 52.

A school is a large group of fish. Schools may have millions of fish in them. Tuna are one kind of fish that live in schools.

segmented body, page 40.

A segmented body is made of separate parts that are joined together. Lobsters and other crustaceans have segmented bodies.

shell, page 82.

A shell is the body covering of a turtle. A shell is made of hard plates and is usually round at the top and flat on the bottom.

skeleton, page 44.

A skeleton is a framework that supports the body of an animal. Coral animals have skeletons.

snout, page 80.

A snout is the part of an animal's head where the nose and mouth are located. Alligators and crocodiles are reptiles with long snouts.

sucker, page 6.

A sucker is a part of an animal's body that attaches to rocks or to the bottom of a stream.

surface current, page 10.

A surface current is an ocean current caused by the wind.

temperate climate, page 20.

A temperate climate is one where winters are cold and summers are warm.

tentacles, page 32.

Tentacles are feelers that grow out of the heads of some invertebrate water animals. Most snails have two tentacles with eyes on them.

toothed whale, page 110.

A toothed whale is a whale that uses teeth to get food. Most whales are toothed whales.

tropical climate, page 20.

A tropical climate is one where it is warm all year.

tusks, page 118.

Tusks are long teeth that grow from the upper jaws of a walrus.

 venom, page 76.

Venom is a strong poison that goes through the fangs of a snake when it bites. Sea snakes use venom to slow down the small fish they feed on.

vertebrae, page 30.

Vertebrae are the bones that make up the backbone. Animals with backbones are called vertebrates.

vertebrate, page 30.

A vertebrate is an animal with a backbone. Some vertebrates, such as fish, turtles, and frogs, live in or around water.

warm-blooded, page 90.

Warm-blooded means that the body temperature of an animal always stays the same, even if the temperature around it changes.

water lily, page 22.

A water lily is a large perennial water plant that grows in lakes, ponds, and slow-moving streams. They are found in both temperate and tropical climates. Water lilies have large, round leaves that float and beautiful flowers.

wing span, page 92.

Wing span is the length of a bird's wings from one tip to the other. The wing span of a gull may be more than 5 feet.

wings, page 90.

Wings are body parts that help birds fly.

Acknowledgments

Illustrations

Kathie Kelleher—**16, 28, 50, 72, 88, 106, 126, 136**
Erika Kors—**10, 12, 18T, 70, 80, 84**
Joe Nerlinger and Lewis Calver—**18B, 52**

Photographs

P.**4 (top)** © Superstock, **(bottom)** © Charles Philip/Westlight; p.**6** © Grant Heilman Photography; p.**20** © Hal Harrison/Grant Heilman Photography; p.**22** Texas Highways; p.**24** © George Laycock/Photo Researchers; p.**26** © Grant Heilman Photography; p.**30** © Robert Hermes/Photo Researchers; p.**32 (top)** © Runk/Schoenberger/Grant Heilman Photography, **(bottom)** California Academy of Sciences; p.**34** © Jeff Rotman/Peter Arnold; p.**36** © Hal Harrison/Grant Heilman Photography; p.**38 (bottom)** © Fred Winner/Photo Researchers, Inc.; p.**40** Texas Highways; p.**42** © Runk/Schoenberger/Grant Heilman Photography; p.**43** © Lawson Wood/CORBIS; p.**44 (left)** National Park Service, **(right)** © R.L Sefton/Bruce Coleman; p.**46 (top)** California Academy of Sciences, **(bottom)** Gary Bell/Taxi/Getty Images; p.**48** National Oceanic and Atmospheric Association; p.**54** © Runk/Schoenberger/Grant Heilman Photography; p.**56 (top)** Texas Parks and Wildlife, **(bottom)** © Runk/Schoenberger/Grant Heilman Photography; p.**58** US Fish and Wildlife Service; p.**62** © Richard Ellis/Photo Researchers; p.**64** National Oceanic and Atmospheric Association; p.**66** Valerie C. Chase/National Aquarium, Baltimore; p.**68** Marineland of Florida; p.**69** Al Giddings/Ocean Images, Inc.; p.**74** © Leonard Lee Rue/Photo Researchers; p.**76** © Brandon D. Cole/CORBIS; p.**78** © Grant Heilman Photography; p.**79 (left)** R. Van Nostrand/Photo Researchers, **(right)** © Fairchild/Peter Arnold; p.**82** © Martin Harvey/CORBIS; p.**86** © Galen Rowell/CORBIS; p.**90 (bottom)** G. Nuechterlein/Vireo; p.**92** Texas Highways; p.**94** ©Zoological Society of San Diego; p.**96** Doug Perrine; p.**98 (top)** ©Zoological Society of San Diego, **(bottom)** E.S. Pethingill, Jr./Vireo; p.**100** J.P. Meyers/Vireo; p.**102** Johann Schumacher/Vireo; p.**104** Texas Parks and Wildlife; p.**108 (top)** California Academy of Sciences, **(bottom)** © Leornard Lee Rue/Photo Researchers; p.**110** Flip Nicklin/Ocean Images, Inc.; p.**112** © Francois Gohier/Photo Researchers; p.**114(bottom)** California Academy of Sciences; p.**116 (top)** Sue Matthews/US Fish and Wildlife Service, **(bottom)** US Fish and Wildlife Service; p.**118** US Fish and Wildlife Service; p.**122** Doug Faulkner/Florida Department of Natural Resources; p.**120 (top)** © Pat and Tom Leeson/Photo Researchers, **(bottom)** © Holt Confer/Grant Heilman Photography; p.**124** Australian News and Information Bureau; p.**128** © Karl H. Maslowski; p.**130 (left)** US Fish and Wildlife Service, **(right)** © Prettyman/PhotoEdit; p.**132** © Bailey/Greenpeace; p.**134** Texas Highways.

Additional photography by Royalty-Free/CORBIS, PhotoDisc/Getty Royalty Free and Photos.com Royalty Free.